Dedication

This book is dedicated to my wife Laura, my children Zara, Peter, Susan and Jenny and to my grandchildren Matthew, Anna and Eve.

Acknowledgements

This book would not have been possible without Neil Thomas. Neil's confidence in my ability to write such a book inspired me to undertake this work.

The following individuals and organisations have also contributed to my work directly and indirectly:

- Peter Drucker
- Tom Peters
- Michael Porter
- Philip Kotler
- Igor Ansoff
- Theodore Levitt
- George Day
- Jagdish Sheth
- Thomas Nagle
- Thorogood
- The Free Press
- The Prentice Hall
- Harvard Business Review
- Management First
- Knowledge Wharton
- Wharton School, University of Pennsylvania

My thanks go to Angela Spall and her production team at Thorogood.

Finally my thanks and love goes to my family, and in particular, my wife Laura, my children Zara, Peter, Susan and Jenny and my grand-children Matthew, Anna and Eve.

About the author

Sultan Kermally is 'Chartered Marketer' and the Fellow of the Chartered Institute of Marketing. He has degrees in geography, economics, sociology and law and Diplomas in marketing, finance and accounting and further education.

He has spent all his professional life in management education and management development. At Management Centre Europe and at the Economist Group, Sultan spent considerable time working directly with management 'gurus' including Peter Drucker, Michael Porter, Philip Kotler, Tom Peters and Richard Pascale, to name but a few.

He has authored eight books including two on managing knowledge.

He can be contacted at: skermally@aol.com

Contents

Introduction   **1**

The relationship between strategy and marketing   2

The influence of the gurus   2

Heavyweight gurus   4

Lightweight gurus   7

Plan of the book   9

ONE   **The fundamentals of marketing**   **11**

The evolution of marketing   11

Key marketing concepts   14

A to Z of marketing   26

TWO   **Peter Drucker**   **29**

Why include him as a marketing guru?   30

Where does Peter Drucker come in?   33

The customer as the decision-maker   35

What do marketing gurus and writers
say about Drucker's contribution to marketing?   37

Drucker's key publications   41

At the feet of Peter Drucker: Lessons learnt   41

THREE	**Theodore Levitt**	**43**
	Marketing myopia	43
	Production Life Cycle	48
	Differentiation	51
	The globalisation of markets	52
	At the feet of Theodore Levitt: Lessons learnt	56
FOUR	**Michael Porter**	**57**
	Porter's Five Forces and marketing	58
	How to conduct competitors' analysis	61
	Porter's Value Chain and marketing	64
	Porter's generic strategies	66
	Differentiation and segmentation	68
	Porter's National Diamond	69
	Porter's key publications	71
	At the feet of Michael Porter: Lessons learnt	72
FIVE	**Philip Kotler**	**73**
	Kotler on marketing management	73
	Importance and nature of marketing	74
	Analysing the market environment	80
	Developing, testing and launching new products and services	82
	Kotler's perspective on strategic marketing	85
	Kotler's key publications	86
	At the feet of Philip Kotler: Lessons learnt	87

SIX	**Tom Peters**	**89**
	Close to the customer	90
	Service obsession	91
	Quality obsession	91
	Nichemanship	92
	Listening to the customers	92
	Closing remarks: A controversy	93
	Peter's on marketing and marketing issues	96
	The pursuit of WOW!	97
	Service with soul	98
	Peter's key publications	103
	At the feet of Tom Peters: Lessons learnt	103
SEVEN	**George Day**	**105**
	Day on strategic marketing planning	105
	His contribution on market-driven strategy	107
	Why do some companies succeed at customer relationship management (and many fail)?	112
	Day's conclusions	114
	The 'Red Queen' syndrome	114
	Day's key publications	116
	At the feet of George Day: Lessons learnt	117
EIGHT	**Jagdish Sheth**	**119**
	Sheth's views on industrial buying decisions	120
	At the feet of Jagdish Sheth: Lessons learnt	125

NINE	**Thomas T. Nagle**	**127**
	Nagle on pricing	127
	At the feet of Thomas Nagle: Lessons learnt	131
TEN	**Gurus and strategic analytical tools**	**133**
	Ansoff's Matrix	133
	Porter's Generic Competitive Strategies	136
	Boston Consulting Group – Product Portfolio Matrix	136
	General Electric Strategic Planning Matrix	139
	Shell Directional Policy Matrix	141
	SWOT (Strengths, Weaknesses, Opportunities and Threats) analysis	142
	Scanning the external environment: (STEP) factors	144
	Scenario planning	147
	Benchmarking	149
ELEVEN	**Further information**	**151**
	Suggested reading	151
	Useful websites	153
	References	154

Introduction

Gurus are management thinkers who have made significant impact on the way management is practised. The word 'guru' is a Hindi word which originates from Sanskrit. It means a teacher and a guide in spiritual matters but in a management context it means a recognised leader in the field.

My first **face-to-face** encounter with management gurus came at Management Centre Europe in Brussels. I became Head of the so-called Guru Division. In fact it was formally called Top Management Division. However, as my predecessor was Shafiq Naz, an Asian from Pakistan and as I, another Asian, succeeded him, it began to be called the Gurus Division – maybe because it was thought that being Asians we would recognise Gurus when we see them!

I was privileged to stage and be 'at the feet of management gurus' including Peter Drucker, Michael Porter, Igor Ansoff, Philip Kotler, Rosabeth Moss Kanter, Gary Hamel, George Day, Tom Peters, Peter Senge, Henry Mintzberg, CK Prahalad, Jagdish Sheth and Tom Nagle, to name but a few.

From my contact I have selected nine gurus (the only guru I have not personally met is Theodore Levitt) and examined their **influence in the field of marketing**. The insights and methods of the gurus can make a big difference to the way organisations are managed.

The relationship between strategy and marketing

There is a strong relationship between corporate strategy and marketing strategy. Corporate strategy is all about deciding the direction the business wants to take. The key questions asked at strategy formulation stage are:

- Where are we now?

- Where do we want to go?

- How do we want to get there?

- What is the timescale involved?

From corporate strategy devolves marketing strategy. Many gurus on strategy, such as Ansoff and Porter, therefore, have made key contributions in the areas of product portfolio analysis, competitive environment and diversification. This book recognises such contribution. Hence **it is about 'gurus on marketing' rather than 'marketing gurus'.**

The influence of the gurus

One of the key attributes of a guru is his/her influence in a specific field of expertise such as management, strategy or marketing. There are 'heavyweight' gurus – those who have made tremendous impact and are well-known internationally – and 'lightweight gurus, those who have made significant impact in a particular field but are not so well-known internationally.

This book considers the following gurus who have made an impact in the field of marketing:

Guru: **Peter Drucker**
Status: Heavyweight guru
Expertise: General Management
Influence: Importance of customers

Guru: **Theodore Levitt**
Status: Heavyweight guru
Expertise: Marketing
Influence: Marketing myopia; product lifecycle; globalisation

Guru: **Philip Kotler**
Status: Heavyweight guru
Expertise: Marketing
Influence: Marketing

Guru: **Michael Porter**
Status: Heavyweight guru
Expertise: Strategy
Influence: Competition; competitive environment

Guru: **Igor Ansoff**
Status: Heavyweight guru
Expertise: Strategic management; strategic thinking
Influence: Strategic marketing

Guru: **Tom Peters**
Status: Heavyweight guru
Expertise: Customers; Management
Influence: Service excellence

Guru: **George Day**
Status: Lightweight guru
Expertise: Strategic marketing
Influence: Value adding for customers

Guru: **Jagdish Sheth**
Status: Lightweight guru
Expertise: Strategic marketing; telecom marketing
Influence: Buyer behaviour

Guru: **Thomas Nagle**
Status: Lightweight guru
Expertise: Strategic pricing
Influence: Strategic pricing in a marketing mix context

Heavyweight gurus

Peter Drucker

Peter Drucker is the guru of all gurus. He is the top thinker in the business world today. He has put 'management discipline' on a very sound footing and has a remarkable ability to spot future trends.

Every student of business management has come across (and if not, must come across) his works. His first book *'Concept of the Corporation'* (1946) was a ground breaking examination of the internal working of General Motors.

He is a professor at Claremont Graduate School in California and consults with various top businesses and governments.

Michael Porter

Michael Porter is the Roland E Christensen professor of business administration at the Harvard Business School. He wrote a landmark work on *'Competitive Strategy: Techniques for Analysing Industries and Competitors'* in 1980. His insights into competition have defined thinking about corporate and national strategies for the past two decades.

His works and influence span many fields including issues related to global competitiveness and problems in healthcare. He is one of the world's most famous business school professors and a sought-after consultant.

Tom Peters

Tom Peters, the co-author of 'In Search of Excellence' (1980), is a very famous management guru. He has a burning passion for service excellence, innovation and leadership.

His books *'Thriving on Chaos'* and *'Liberation Management'* became bestsellers as soon as they were published. In the first one he preached management revolution and in the second he celebrated the death of middle management. He is completely different from other heavyweight gurus. According to Charles Handy, a management guru himself:

> *'It isn't his colourful style, his flair for self-promotion or his frenetic energy on the platform... He has a knack for getting under an organisation's skin.'*

Igor Ansoff

Dr Igor Ansoff was one of the first gurus to recognise the need for the concept of strategic management. He served as a professor of Industrial Administration in the Graduate School at Carnegie-Mellon University, Professor of Management at Vanderbilt University, Nashville, Tennessee and a Professor at the European Institute for Advanced Studies in Management, Brussels, Belgium.

He has written numerous books and published many articles on the subject of strategic management. He has been a consultant to companies like General Electric, Philips and IBM.

All students of strategy and marketing are conversant with his matrix – the Ansoff's matrix.

Theodore Levitt

Theodore Levitt was Edward W Carter Professor of Business Administration Emeritus at the Harvard Business School and a former editor of the Harvard Business Review. Professor Levitt provided an insight into the importance of marketing during the period when most organisations were production oriented. His article 'Marketing Myopia' which appeared in the Harvard Business Review in 1960 was his landmark article which made him a marketing guru.

He has authored numerous articles on economics, management and marketing subjects. He is a four-time winner of the McKinsey Awards competitions for best annual article in the Harvard Business Review; winner of the John Hancock Award for Excellence in Business Journalism in 1969; recipient of the Charles Coolidge Parlin Award as 'Marketing Man of the Year', 1970; recipient of the George Gallup Award for Marketing Excellence, 1976; recipient of the 1978 Paul D Converse Award of the American Marketing Association for major contributions to marketing; recipient of the 1989 William M McFeeley Award of the International Management Council for major contribution to management.

Philip Kotler

Philip Kotler is the most well-known and pre-eminent thinker on marketing. He is SC Johnson and Son Distinguished Professor of International Marketing at the JL Kellogg Graduate School of Management, Northwestern University.

He is the author of the most widely used marketing book in leading business schools worldwide, *'Marketing Management: Analysis, Planning Implementation and Control'* (published 1967 and now in its 10th edition). The book was named by the Financial Times as 'one of the 50 top business books of all time'. He was the first recipient of the American Marketing Associations Distinguished Marketing Educator Award in 1995.

He is an influential corporate consultant and a global marketing guru. His most recent book is *'Kotler on Marketing: How to Create, Win and Dominate Markets'*.

Lightweight gurus

George Day

George Day is a Professor of Marketing at the Wharton School, University of Pennsylvania. He has held visiting professorships at The London Business School, Massachusetts Institute of Technology and Harvard University.

He advises business, government and research organisations on marketing management, strategic planning and competitive strategies. He coined the term *'market-driven strategy'* nearly a decade ago – in a conference and a book by that name. His influence has been in positioning marketing at the heart of strategy process.

Jagdish Sheth

Jagdish Sheth was a Professor of Marketing at the University of Southern California; Distinguished Professor at the University of Illinois and at the Massachusetts Institute of Technology. Currently he is the Charles H Kellstadt Professor of Marketing at the Goizueta Business School, Emory University.

He has published extensively. His book, which he co-authored with John A Howard, 'The Theory of Buyer Behaviour' (1969), is a classic in the field.

He has been rated as one of the top ten marketing professors in the country in a survey of marketing professionals. His areas of influence are global marketing, global competition, telecom marketing and strategic thinking. He is a distinguished educator, author, speaker and senior management advisor.

Thomas Nagle

Thomas Nagle is a Professor of Marketing at Boston University and a President of Strategic Pricing Group, Boston, Massachusetts

He earns his place in the 'guru table' because of his work and influence in positioning the subject of pricing at strategic level and within the context of the marketing mix concept.

Plan of the book

The book begins by exploring key concepts and frameworks in marketing. It is presented in a format of 'Marketing in a Nutshell'.

The reader is reminded of the key concepts in marketing so that when he/she comes to read about contributions made by various gurus he/she can position the concepts and frameworks within the marketing discipline.

At the end of each chapter a checklist is presented to highlight the salient lessons learnt from each guru.

ONE
The fundamentals of marketing

The evolution of marketing

Marketing has gone through various schools of thought. In the beginning marketing was primarily concerned with producing products to satisfy consumer wants. It was very much influenced by Economics discipline in that it focused its attention on economic exchanges to satisfy consumer wants. According to Adam Smith's *'Wealth of Nations'* (1776), *'Consumption is the sole end and purpose of production....'* This was referred to as **'the commodity school of thought'**.

During the commodity school of thought era, goods were classified as 'convenience goods', 'emergency goods', 'shopping lines'. This classification and subsequent fine-tuning and additions (introduction of preference goods) went on from 1912 through 1980s. In 1986 Murphy and Enis[1] introduced the following categories of products:

- Convenience products
- Preference products
- Shopping products
- Speciality products

In the 1950s many marketing theorists began to advocate a more managerial-based approach; thus began **the managerial school of marketing**. According to Sheth:[2]

> 'Then marketing, like economics, became 'managerial' by which I mean that marketing became the job of a manager; this in turn led to the concept of the four 'Ps' of marketing.'

In 1960 Theodore Levitt published his ground breaking article in the Harvard Business Review entitled 'Marketing Myopia' (see Chapter three).

Levitt advocated shifting the focus on marketing from product-orientation to customer-orientation'. During this period came the introduction of marketing mix, **the four Ps** of marketing, namely **product, place, price and promotion**, introduced by Neil Borden. Marketing myopia and marketing mix seem to be the key elements of the managerial school of thought. While Levitt was advocating marketing as *'providing customer creating satisfactions'*, other writers in the field were introducing a concept of segmentation to facilitate satisfying needs of different groups of customers.

The next stage was **the buying behaviour school of thought**. The advocates of this school focused their attention on the behaviour of consumers in relation to their buying decisions. Researches were being conducted on motivational and psychological factors affecting buying behaviour in the 1950s but they were not incorporated in marketing 'discipline' till later on. The influential consumer behaviour model was that of John Howard and **Jagdish Sheth** (1969).

In the 1970s numerous researches were being conducted on industrial and organisational buying behaviour ranging from profit to not-for-profit organisations.

Kotler[3] then advocated the importance of values in the exchange process which facilitated the transfer of goods from producers to consumers. He believed that the exchange process involved not only goods and money but also time, energy and feelings. Other writers at that time were also emphasising the 'social' nature of exchange. Thus came into existence **the social exchange school of thought**.

Since 1990s customers became the focus of attention. From Levitt right through to George Day the emphasis of marketing practice has been to transform organisations into customer-driven business. We are now in the era of **'service excellence school of thought'**.

Marketing discipline therefore, is heavily influenced by economics, psychology, philosophy, management and other social sciences.

We will in this book look at the work of some of the marketing gurus such as Levitt, Kotler, Sheth and Day and some other gurus on strategy such as Ansoff, Porter and Peters whose works have direct bearings on the practice of marketing.

Key marketing concepts

What is marketing?

The Chartered Institute of Marketing in the UK defines marketing as:

> *...The management process responsible for identifying, anticipating and satisfying customer requirements profitably.'*

Marketing is defined as the anticipation, management, and satisfaction of demand through the exchange process.

According to Kotler[4], marketing is a:

> *'...Process by which individuals and groups obtain what they need and want by creating and exchanging products and value for others.'*

> *'Exchange processes involve work. Sellers must search for buyers, identify their needs, design good products, and promote them... and set prices for them. Activities such as product development, research, communication, distribution, pricing, and service are core marketing activities. '*

The Marketing Mix

The marketing mix involves the four Ps of marketing. These four Ps are product, price, place and promotion.

PRODUCT

The product can be tangibles such as cars, furniture, food or intangibles such as service at hotels, or service provided by professionals such as consultants, nurses, lawyers or doctors.

Characteristics of service

They are: Intangible, perishable, inseparable and specific/variable.

Product aspect involves what to produce, the quality of the product, packaging, branding, design, colour, presentation and so on.

Note: For different attributes associated with core product refer to Differentiation article by Theodore Levitt in Chapter three.

PRICE

What price to charge; discounts available; special offers. The pricing of a product should be considered very carefully and it should be considered not from the cost point of view but from the marketing point of view. This aspect is dealt with by Thomas Nagle, guru of strategic pricing, in Chapter nine.

PLACE

This aspect incorporates selling through distributors or directly (the internet now facilitates selling directly); warehousing, storage, the types of outlets; tele-selling or selling on-line.

PROMOTION

This incorporates advertising, publicity, the image to pursue, personal selling, and the choice of media, (newspaper, radio or TV advert).

The object of promotion is to create **awareness, interest, desire and action – A.I.D.A. principle**.

The four elements of marketing mix must be blended effectively to target particular segments. For example, if you consider the introduction of Four-In-One printer Lexmark X75 which is a printer, scanner and copier and fax machine, it is normally sold at about £139 but the launch price was £95; it is advertised via various catalogues (Argos, Staples); it can be purchased at stores or by on-line.

It is presented as an integrated product, value for money, space saving and cost-effective.

Marketing mix checklist – some guidelines

PRODUCT

- What does your product do and what does it offer?
- Do you have a brand and what does it stand for?
- Determine quality, design, packaging and presentation.
- What are the intangible elements of the product/service?
- How can you augment your product.
- What other value can you add to core product?

PRICE

- Consider the level of price – price sensitivity; competitors' price, discounts.
- Assess psychological aspects of price.
- What policy you are going to adopt in terms of different categories of buyers?
- Integrate pricing policy with other aspects of marketing mix.

PLACE

- Do you have a website and are you willing to sell on-line?
- Direct selling v. selling through distributors.
- Consider customer preferences.
- Consider logistics – transport, distribution.

PROMOTION

- What type of promotion you have in mind.
- Do you want to advertise via bill posters or radio or newspaper or television?
- Is it appropriate to the segment you are addressing?

- Consider the promotion budget.

- What resources you are willing to allocate.

Nowadays some writers emphasise on focusing on marketing mix from the customers' perspective. **The four Ps – product, price, place and promotion is from the perspective of what the supplier does. To consider the marketing mix from the perspective of the customer one needs to consider the customer value, cost to customer, convenience and communication.**

Selling v. Marketing

According to Theodore Levitt[5], marketing guru:

> 'Selling focuses on the needs of the seller, marketing on the needs of the buyer. Selling is preoccupied with the seller's need to convert his product into cash, marketing with the idea of satisfying the needs of the customer by means of the product and the whole cluster of things associated with creating, delivering and finally consuming it.'

Selling benefits

Experts in marketing advocate selling benefits to customers rather than praising the attributes of the product or service. What benefits would customers gain by acquiring the product or service.

Market segmentation

A market is subdivided into sub-markets known as segments. The heterogeneous market is divided into homogeneous divisions or groups. Marketing segmentation can be done on the basis of geographic, demographic, and socio-psychological factors.

Geographic factors

Which countries or regions do you want to market your products in? Consider population size and density; population traits; cities, villages etc.

Demographic factors

Population size, density, traits, composition, structure, family size, and other variables can be used to segment the market.

Socio-psychological factors

What do consumers think of the products in terms of their life-style; their attitude; social class; brand loyalty; personality types; health factors etc.

For segmentation to be successful it is important for a segment to be large enough for it to be profitable; **distinct** enough to differentiate; **homogeneous** enough to prepare a marketing plan and **measurable** to determine the effectiveness of marketing.

Segmentation is important in developing a target marketing plan. For marketing strategy to succeed, segmentation has to be meaningful and appropriate.

Product/service positioning

Once the segment is determined then a decision has to be made as to how to position the product. The idea of positioning is to find out how the customers/consumers in particular segments are going to perceive your product/service and your message about these products and service.

It is said that: *'what consumers perceive, consumers should receive'*.

For example, if an organisation is providing an off-shore tax service it has to decide how to position its service among rich people (high net worth individuals as they are referred to by professionals).

Product lifecycle

A product goes through various stages in its life starting from an introduction stage to maturity and decline. Different stages generate different revenues and profits depending on the marketing strategies and plans adopted. (This aspect is highlighted in Chapter three under the contribution made by Theodore Levitt.)

Product portfolio analysis

There are various ways of managing a range of products (portfolio of products). The simplest way is applying Pareto's Law – identifying the 20 per cent of your products producing 80 per cent of total profits.

There are other ways of deciding on product portfolio. They include General Electric Model, Ansoff's Matrix, Boston Consulting Group. These techniques are the subject matter of chapter ten.

Branding

Brands are developed by all types of organisations and take many forms. Brand is defined as:

> 'A distinctive identity that differentiates a relevant, enduring and credible promise of value associated with a product, or service or organisation and indicates the source of that promise.[6]'

According to Philip Kotler (*'Principles of Marketing'*), it is:

> *'A name term, sign, symbol or design or a combination of these intended to identify the goods or services of one seller or a group of sellers and to differentiate them from those of competitors.'*

Brands are intangible assets of organisations. Brands like Unilever, IBM, Microsoft, and Sony etc. have market values that exceed their book values.

There are manufacturer brands (Heinz), dealer or distributor brands (Sainsbury's), and generic brands that contain the names of the products (Scotch tape).

According to Evans and Berman,[7] branding eases product identification, assures customers of a level of quality, and performs other valuable functions.

Advantages of strong branding

- Allows companies to charge a premium price.
- Commands marketing channel space.
- Indicates high quality.
- Facilitates consumer buying decision-making process.
- Facilitates market positioning.
- Constitutes barrier to entry.

Brand is considered to be a legal instrument, a logo, a company, an identity, a consumer perception, a personality, or a relationship. It, therefore, has many perspectives.

Brand extension

Brand extension is a strategy by which an established brand name is applied to new products. An example here would be the 'Virgin' brand' applying to trains and financial services.

Brand loyalty

To get consumers to become loyal to brands it is important to understand their needs and aspirations and then manipulating this knowledge to develop brands. Loyalty cards by various organisations are designed to establish loyalty.

Trademark is a brand or a symbol that has legal protection.

Marketing information

Successful marketing depends on gathering information and using this information. Information is obtained by conducting researches and surveys.

Market research involves getting information on **markets** (size and trends, composition and nature of markets, distribution patterns, buying practices etc); on **competitors** and **customers**.

Consumer behaviour

For marketing to be effective it is important to understand how consumers make decisions associated with their purchases.

Consumer behaviour is influenced by numerous factors. These are psychological factors, social factors and economic factors. Understanding of the impact and influence of these factors help marketers understand buyers' purchasing behaviour.

Analysis of consumer behaviour and associated response will enable organisations to adopt consumer-oriented marketing.

Service excellence

In the past two decades many writers have emphasised the value and the importance of satisfying customers and providing service excellence to win and maintain competitive advantage. One of the attributes of the excellent companies mentioned by Peters and Waterman[8] was staying close to customers. (See Chapter six) However, some gurus (see George Day Chapter seven) warn against staying too close to customers.

Marketing environment

Businesses operate within the context of macro-environment. The factors operating in the macro-environment could be categorised as sociological or social, technological, economic and political. These are generally referred to as S.T.E.P. factors.

Changes in the step factors have a knock-on effect on corporate strategy. Therefore, it is very important in formulating corporate strategy and associated marketing strategy that notice is taken of the changes in the macro-economic environment and the impact these changes could have on your business (see Chapter ten).

Competitive environment

In addition to taking note of and analysing macro-environment it is also important to scan and assess the competitive environment. The popular framework used here is that presented by Professor Michael Porter 'The Five Forces Framework'. (See chapter four.)

Assessing the competitive environment involves looking at barriers to entry and exist; availability of substitutes; buying power of sellers and buyers, and the intensity of competition.

Marketing strategy

Marketing strategy should be aligned with corporate strategy. Marketing strategy should articulate actions and activities that would identify and evaluate the threats and challenges facing organisations and the determining and targeting of market segments to achieve strategic objectives.

In chapter ten we look at various techniques used to determine the appropriate market strategies.

Market planning

Marketing planning involves setting marketing goals and the action plan to achieve these goals. The plan provides the structure and a mechanism for managerial decisions.

Organisations formulate strategies and from these strategies strategic objectives are formulated. These objectives relate to financial goals (e.g. return on investment, asset utilisation, gross margins etc.) marketing goals (market share, market growth, customer base etc.) employee goals (staff turnover; skills etc.).

Prior to formulating these strategies the organisation should undertake a SWOT (strengths, weaknesses, opportunities and threats) analysis (see chapter ten) and undertake an external environmental scanning.

From various analyses, identify opportunities to achieve marketing objectives set. The organisation should consider its chosen segments, determine marketing mix, set budgets, and start implementing the plan. Since the business world is dynamic by nature, the marketing objectives should constantly be monitored and measured.

The strategic aspect of planning is related to corporate planning. The day-to-day marketing activities constitute operational aspects of marketing planning.

According to Malcolm McDonald[9]:

> 'A recent study of leading companies carried out by Cranfield showed that a marketing plan should contain:
>
> - A summary of all the principal external factors which affected the company's marketing performance during the previous year, together with a statement of the company's strengths and weaknesses vis-à-vis the competition. This is what we call a SWOT (i.e. strengths, weaknesses, opportunities and threats) analysis.
>
> - Some assumptions about the key determinants of marketing success and failure.
>
> - Overall marketing objectives and strategies.
>
> - Programmes containing details of timing, responsibilities and costs, with sales forecasts and budgets.'

Globalisation and global marketing

Globalisation is transforming the fundamental structures and nature of international trade. The process of globalisation influences the way we trade, our trading partners, the skills required to compete in an environment, the innovation of organisation, labour mobility, and cultures and values.

The collapse of communism and almost universal support for market economies, combined with accelerated technological developments and explosion of information, have encouraged a far greater trend towards globalisation than before.

Writing on 'The Globalisation of Markets' Theodore Levitt[10], says:

> *'Commercially, nothing confirms this so much as the booming success of McDonald's everywhere from the Champs Elysees to the Ginza, of Coca-Cola in Bahrain and Pepsi in Moscow, and of rock music, Greek salad, Hollywood movies, Revlon cosmetics, Sony televisions, and Levi jeans everywhere...'*

According to Warren J. Keegan[11]:

'The foundation for a successful global marketing program is a sound understanding of the marketing discipline. Marketing is a process of focusing the resources and objectives of an organisation on environmental opportunities and needs. The first and most fundamental fact about marketing is that it is a universal discipline. The marketing discipline is equally applicable from Australia to Zanzibar, from the United States to Japan. Marketing is a set of concepts, tools, theories, practices and procedures, and experience. Together these elements constitute a teachable and learnable body of knowledge.'

'Global marketing is the process of focusing the resources and objectives of a company on global marketing opportunities. Companies engage in global marketing for two reasons: to take advantage of opportunities for growth and expansion, and to survive. Companies that fail to pursue global opportunities are likely to eventually lose their domestic markets because they will be pushed aside by stronger and more competitive global competitors.... Global marketing's importance today is shaped by the dynamic interplay of several driving and restraining forces. The former include market needs and wants, technology, transportation improvements, costs, quality, global peace, world economic growth, and recognition of opportunities to develop leverage by operating globally. Restraining forces include market differences, management myopia, organisational culture, and national controls.'

A to Z of marketing

A   Align your marketing strategy with corporate or organisational strategy.

B   Buyer behaviour at individual as well as collective level should be considered seriously.

C   Communicate your marketing objectives externally as well as internally.

D   Differentiate your products and service to win and maintain competitive advantage.

E   Environmental scanning should be undertaken to identify your opportunities and challenges.

F   Focus on monitoring, measuring and adjusting your marketing objectives.

G   Globalise, if necessary, but keep local needs in perspective.

H   Have the courage of your convictions.

I   Information on your competitors and customers should be converted into organisational knowledge.

J   Juggle with various marketing mix components to consolidate your segmentation strategy.

K   Knowledge of your customers and competitors, if used effectively, gives you a competitive edge.

L   Listen to your customers and partners.

M   Measure your performance, manage your marketing activities and motivate your staff.

N   Non-financial measures are just as important as financial measures.

O   Operational marketing planning should be part of your strategic marketing planning.

P   People (staff and customers), processes and products should be monitored continuously to maintain your marketing performance.

Q   Quality should be the primary consideration affecting all aspects of your business.

R   Relationship marketing should be actively encouraged.

S   Service excellence should be the core message of your organisation.

T   Transform your organisation into a market-driven one.

U   Understand the true nature of marketing.

V   Value chain should help you create value for your customers.

W   Winning competitive advantage is not enough; you have to sustain it.

Y   Your conviction, commitment and communication in relation to marketing will bring you success.

Z   Zeal and zest of your staff should be nurtured to create marketing mindset.

TWO
Peter Drucker

Peter Drucker is the father of management gurus; he is the guru of all gurus. When he speaks most CEOs pay attention. He was born in Vienna in 1909 and trained in Economics. He has subsequently become the world's foremost pioneer of management theory.

He is a teacher, consultant, writer and a speaker and has become the leading management gurus of his time. His first book 'Concept of the Corporation' (1946) was a ground breaking examination of the internal workings of General Motors.

His management books, 'The Practice of Management' (1954), 'Management: Tasks Responsibilities, Practices' (1973), 'Innovation and Entrepreneurship' (1985), 'The Frontiers of Management' (1986) and his recent books 'Peter Drucker on the Profession of Management' (1998) and 'Management Challenges for the 21st Century' (1999) have become international bestsellers.

He popularised concepts such as 'privatisation', 'management by objectives', decentralisation', 'knowledge worker' and 'the knowledge economy' – concepts which we now take for granted.

He is a professor of Social Sciences and Management at the Claremont Graduate University, California which named its Graduate School of Management after him. In July 2002, President George Bush presented him with the Presidential Medal of Freedom, the Nation's highest civilian honour.

According to 'The Witch Doctors' (1996)[12]:

> 'In most areas of intellectual life nobody can quite decide on who the top dog is – sometimes because rival schools of thought have rival champions, sometimes because there are so many fine specimens to choose from. In the world of management gurus, however, there is no debate. Peter Drucker is one management guru to whom other management gurus kowtow. He is also one of the few thinkers from any discipline who can reasonably claim to have changed the world... but Drucker is the one management theorist who every tolerably well-educated person, however contemptuous of business or infuriated by jargon, really ought to read.'

Why include him as a marketing guru?

Peter Drucker is an all-rounder guru. Before Theodore Levitt, Drucker was the only management writer who emphasised the importance of marketing and the importance of the customer.

In the 1960s and 1970s marketing was defined very narrowly focusing attention on flows of goods from producers to consumers. The following are some examples of definitions of marketing at that time:

- Marketing is the process of determining consumer demand and facilitating sales to ultimate consumers.

- Marketing is creating utility of time and place.

- Marketing consists of the activities of buying, selling, transporting and storing goods.

- Marketing is the performance of activities which seek to achieve an organisation's objectives.

Most of the definitions focused marketing activities towards organisations production processes. Marketing was conceived as a process the context of which was economic exchanges in the marketplace.

The thinking was heavily influenced by Adam Smith who in his 'Wealth of Nations', published in 1776, wrote: *'Consumption is the sole end and purpose of production.'*

Organisations were very much product and production oriented. The author remembers a discussion he had in the early 1970s with some manufacturing managers of a well-branded white goods company. They emphasised it was important for them to produce goods that they felt should be produced and not waste time asking consumers about their opinions. If the consumers do not buy their goods then it was their loss! The company should make every effort to sell these goods. Such was the prevailing attitude in the 1960s and 1970s. It was against such background that Professor Levitt wrote his landmark article 'Marketing Myopia' which is discussed in detail in Chapter two.

Most organisations equated marketing with selling. According to Professor Levitt[13]:

> *'The difference between marketing and selling is more than semantic. Selling focuses on the needs of the seller, marketing on the needs of the buyer. Selling is preoccupied with the seller's need to convert his product into cash, marketing with the idea of satisfying the needs of the customer by means of the product and the whole cluster of things associated with creating, delivering, and finally consuming it.'*

Joel R. Evans and Barry Berman, (1982) in their book 'Marketing' (Collier Macmillan) highlight the following differences between selling and marketing:

Selling

- Sales-oriented.
- Output 'sold' to consumers.
- One-way process.
- Short-run goals.
- Volume-oriented.
- Emphasis on single consumers.
- Narrow view of consumer needs.
- Informal planning and feedback.
- Little adaptation to environment.

Marketing

- Consumer-oriented.
- Marketing research determines output.
- Two-way process (interactive).
- Long-term goals.
- Profit-oriented.
- Emphasis on groups of consumers.
- Broad view of consumer needs.
- Integrated planning and feedback.
- Appropriate adaptation to environment.

Where does Peter Drucker come in?

Since 1954 Peter Drucker has been writing about the importance of focusing on customers in order to achieve the purpose of business. Consider the following extracts from his books.

In chapter six of his book '*The Practice of Management*', Peter Drucker asks: 'What is our business – and what should it be?' He writes:

> 'What is our business if not determined by the producer, but by the consumer. It is not defined by the company's name, statutes or article of corporation, but by the want the customer satisfies when he buys a product or a service. The question can therefore be answered only by looking at the business from the outside, from the point of view of the customer and the market. What the customer sees, thinks, believes and wants at any given time must be accepted by management as an objective fact deserving to be taken as seriously as the reports of the salesman, the tests of the engineer or the figures of the accountant – something few in management find it easy to do. And management must make a conscious effort to get honest answers from the consumer himself rather than attempt to read his mind.'
>
> 'The first step towards finding out what our business is, is to raise the question: 'Who is the customer'? – The actual and the potential customer? Where is he? How does he buy? How can he be reached?'

Drucker also advocates being proactive and asking questions in relation to future growth. Management must ask 'What will our business be'? To answer this question requires paying attention to the following four factors:

1 Market potential and market trend.

2 Changes in the market structure.

3 Innovations.

4 Unsatisfied consumer wants.

The answers should be based on the definition of the market that is customer oriented.

> 'If we want to know a business we have to start with its purpose... There is only one valid definition of business purpose: to create a customer.'

> 'It is a customer who determines what a business is. For it is the customer and he alone, who through being willing to pay for a good or for a service, converts economic resources into wealth, things into goods. What the business thinks it produces is not of first importance – especially not to the future of the business and to its success. What the customer thinks he is buying, what he considers 'value' is decisive – it determines what a business is, what it produces and whether it will prosper.'

> 'The customer is the foundation of a business and keeps it in existence. He alone gives employment. And it is to supply the consumer that society entrusts wealth-producing resources to the business enterprise.'

> 'Actually marketing is so basic that it is not just enough to have a strong sales department and to entrust marketing to it. Marketing is not only much broader than selling; it is not a specialised activity at all. It encompasses the entire business. It is the whole business seen from the point of view of the final result that is from the customer's point of view. Concern and responsibility for marketing must therefore permeate all areas of the enterprise.'

Source: Drucker, Peter (1954). 'The Practice of Management'. Heinemann Professional Publishing.

The customer as the decision-maker

> *'Specifically, there are no results within the organisation. All the results are on the outside. The only business results, for instance, are produced by a customer who converts the costs and efforts of the business into revenues and profits through his willingness to exchange his purchasing power for the products or services of the business. The customer may make his decisions as a consumer on the basis of market considerations of supply and demand, or as a socialist government which regulates supply and demand on the basis of essentially non-economic value preferences. In either case the decision-maker is outside rather than inside the business.'*

Source: *Drucker, Peter. (1966). 'The Effective Executive'. Heinemann.*

Writing on the subject of innovation and entrepreneurship[14], he suggested knowledge-based innovation adopt a market focus.

> *'Knowledge-based innovation can aim at creating the market for its products. This is what DuPont did with Nylon. It did not 'sell' Nylon; it created a consumer market for women's hosiery and women's underwear using Nylon, a market for automobile tyres using Nylon, and so on. It then delivered Nylon to the fabricators to make the articles for which DuPont had already created a demand for which in effect it had already sold.'*

For a new venture to succeed there is a need for market focus. It must anticipate new market needs and potential competitors. He gives the examples of products such as Xerox copiers, DDT, 3M Scotch Tape, computers; the products which were designed for specific segment users, mainly industrial. No one could foresee the use of these products by household consumers.

Drucker makes the point that it is difficult to undertake market research which is a typical textbook prescription for new products. Such market researches are made on narrow assumptions.

> 'The new venture therefore needs to start out with the assumption that its product or service may find customers in markets no one thought of, for uses no one envisaged when the product or service was designed, and that it will be bought by customers outside its field of vision and even unknown to the new venture.'

The new product requires marketing focus that includes anticipating new markets and new competitors and willingness to take risks to experiment. Drucker makes the point that a 'product 'or a 'service' is defined by the customer, not by the producer. Such an outlook makes a venture market-oriented rather than product oriented.

> 'The greatest danger for the new venture is to 'know better' than the customer what the product or service is, or should be, how it should be bought, and what it should be used for. And it needs to accept that elementary axiom of marketing: businesses are not paid to reform customers. They are paid to satisfy customers.'

Creative imitators of products, according to Drucker, are not innovators as such. They try to study the markets and the customers; thus becoming market focused and market-driven. One of the key strategies for organisations to gain and sustain competitive advantage is to stop their competitors imitating them. To do so these organisations have to serve their existing market and consumers better than their potential competitors. Creative imitators become successful because they satisfy the existing markets better than pioneers of products.

What do marketing gurus and writers say about Drucker's contribution to marketing?

On the concept of marketing

T. LEVITT

'Marketing Myopia' was not intended as an analysis or even prescription; it was intended as a manifesto. It did not pretend to take a balanced position. Nor was it a new idea – Peter Drucker... had each done more original and balanced work on 'the marketing concept'. My scheme, however, tied marketing more closely to the inner orbit of business policy. Drucker – especially in 'The Concept of the Corporation' and the 'Practice of Management' – originally provided me with a great deal of insight.'

Source: Theodore. Levitt (1983) 'The Marketing Imagination'.

Marketing and less developed countries

The economic literature places a great deal of emphasis on the role of 'marketing' in economic development when marketing is defined as distribution. Drucker in his article 'Marketing and Economic Development' (Journal of Marketing, January, 1958) argues 'that experience in the distributive sector is valuable because it generates a pool of entrepreneurial talent in a society where alternatives for such training are scarce.'

Source: Warren J. Keegan (1984). 'Multinational Marketing Management'. Prentice Hall.

On market research

'As Peter Drucker has pointed out, the failure of American companies to successfully commercialise fax machines – an American innovation – can be traced to research that indicated no potential demand for such a product. The problem, in Drucker's view, stems from the typical survey question for a product targeted at a latent market. Suppose a researcher asks, 'Would you buy a telephone accessory that costs upwards of $1,500 and enables you to send, for $1 a page, the same letter the post office delivers for 25 cents?' On the basis of economics alone, the respondent most likely will answer 'No'.

Drucker explains that the reason Japanese companies are the leading sellers of fax machines today is that their understanding of the market was not based on survey research. Instead they reviewed the early days of mainframe computers, photocopy machines, cellular telephones, and other information and communications products. The Japanese realised that, judging only by the initial economics of buying and using these new products, the prospects of market acceptance were low. Yet, each of these products became hugely successful after people began to use them. This realisation prompted the Japanese to focus on the market for the benefits provided by fax machines, rather than the market for the machines themselves.'

Source: Keegan, Warren, J. (1974). 'Global Marketing Management'. Prentice Hall.

Role of marketing

'...Peter Drucker has long counselled that the role of marketing is innovation and the creation of new markets. Innovation begins with abandonment of the old and obsolete. In Drucker's words:

'Innovative organisations spend neither time nor resources on defending yesterday. Systematic abandonment of yesterday alone can transfer resources... for work on the new.'

Source: Keegan, Warren J. '(1974). 'Global Marketing Management'. Prentice Hall.

Writers on marketing since Drucker began to broaden the concept of marketing and to shift the emphasis from producers to customers.

Marketing today is about focusing on customers' needs, their preferences and satisfying these needs. The modern definition of marketing focuses on consumers. It is defined as anticipation, management and satisfaction of demand through the exchange process.

This involves undertaking consumer research, understanding consumer buying behaviour, thinking about the ways to reach consumers, to satisfy existing consumer needs and to anticipate future needs. Marketing and its focus on meeting and anticipating customer needs is now generally accepted as a key business and marketing philosophy.

Sigmund and D'Amico (1984) in their book 'Marketing' (John Wiley) write:

> 'Consumer orientation is the first aspect of the marketing concept. The consumer or customer should be seen as 'the fulcrum, the pivot point about which the business moves in operating for the balanced interests of all concerned'. Organisations that have accepted the marketing concept try to create products and services with the customers' needs in mind. It follows that first determination must be what the customer wants. The marketing concept rightly suggests that it is better to find out what the customer wants and offer that product, than it is to make a product and then try to sell it to somebody.'

> 'Product success, industry leadership, even corporate survival, depends on satisfying the consumer. When a company defines the broad nature of its business it must take a consumer-oriented perspective. When setting a corporate mission the company's style, its direction, and its goals, the company must avoid short-sighted narrow-minded thinking that will lead it to define its purpose from a product orientation rather than a consumer orientation.'

Consider this with what Peter Drucker wrote in his book 'Practice of Management' published in 1954.

The consumer aspect has been well integrated in marketing concept and technological developments and convergence of technology are facilitating sophisticated approach to gathering information on customers.

According to Professor David Schmittlein,[15] of Wharton School, new technology and new approaches to marketing are allowing companies to collect, analyse and use information about their customers. He writes:

'For many companies, the benefits of managing customers as strategic assets (MCSA) have been great. They include more loyal customers, who are less inclined to shop around or buy on price, more efficient, effective and highly targeted communications programmes, reactivation of very profitable 'lost' customers at low cost, and more focused and successful development of new products.'

'Customers who have chosen a company's products or services tend to develop assets of characteristics that are important and advantageous to the company. These include awareness of the breath of its products, familiarity with their specific performance characteristics, and accommodation of them into a lifestyle or self-image or (for business customers) into established operating procedures.'

'The major elements in the strategic use of customer assets begins with the assembly of a market-oriented customer database including marketing programme contacts with the customer, a transaction history (inquiries, order payment), merged with any customer service information, available geodemographic descriptions, media habits and any responses to surveys that may be relevant. From this information, segmentation of the customer base is a critical step assembling groups of customers most appropriate for highly customised marketing programmes that may include cross-selling, new product development (including mass customisation in some cases), design and timing of customised communication programmes, and (in the case of apparently lapsed customers) reactivation programmes'.

Some organisations now use very sophisticated technology to gather information on customers and transform this information into knowledge which enables them to win and sustain competitive advantage.

Drucker's key publications

- 'The Practice of Management' (1955). Heinemann.

- 'The Effective Executive' (1967). Heinemann.

At the feet of Peter Drucker: Lessons learnt

- Business is marketing and marketing is business.

- Business should be defined from the customers' perspective.

- Customers decide the nature of business.

- Profits are generated by customers.

- Business should learn to create markets.

- Market focus determines the success of business.

- Broaden the assumptions when conducting market research.

- Businesses are not placed to reform customers but to satisfy customers.

- Innovation involves abandonment of the old and obsolete.

- For marketing to succeed focus on benefits.

THREE
Theodore Levitt

On marketing myopia, product life cycle, differentiation and globalisation of markets.

Theodore Levitt published many articles. Nine of the key articles from the Harvard Business Review were reproduced in his book '*Marketing Imagination*' published by Collier Macmillan, London 1983.

The following four articles have been singled out to reflect the impact of Levitt's influence on marketing as marketing guru.

Marketing myopia

This was Professor Levitt's landmark article following his experience at Standard Oil. In formulating business strategy the fundamental question posed is 'what business are we in?' In answering this question most organisations focus on industry as opposed to the markets. Such a focus makes an organisation production-focused as opposed to market-focused.

In his article Levitt argues that the railroads stopped growing not because the need for passengers and freight stopped growing. The business suffered because it was very narrowly defined. It considered itself to be in railroads business rather than transport business.

Hollywood suffered because it defined its business very narrowly. It thought it was in the movie business when it was actually in the entertainment business.

He gives the examples of many other businesses such as dry cleaning, grocery stores, and electronic utilities, all of which have suffered because of the narrow definition of business which did not extend to consumer needs.

Defining the business in terms of its capabilities rather than market needs makes it production-oriented. The business should be defined according to consumer needs and demands.

He gives the example of two successful companies DuPont and Corning Glass Works. According to Levitt, these businesses focus their strategies on their product capabilities but these capabilities are constantly reviewed and enhanced in order to take on board changing customer needs.

He writes:

> 'It is constant watchfulness for opportunities to apply their technical know-how to the creation of customer-satisfying uses which accounts for their prodigious output of successful new products. Without a very sophisticated eye on the customer, most of their new products might have been wrong, their sales methods useless.'[16]

He argues that growth in much business is threatened due to lack of marketing imagination at the top management level. He declared that there was not a growth industry as such. There were merely growth opportunities which business had to take into consideration and capitalise on by adapting their own capabilities.

He put forward four conditions which led to business failures. These are:

1   The belief that growth comes about by increasing population and increasing affluence. Population growth increases the market for the product and businesses adjust their supplies to meet demand. There was no need for a business to think imaginatively or innovatively as long as they are not faced with a problem.

He wrote:

'If thinking is an intellectual response to a problem, then the absence of a problem leads to the absence of thinking. If your product has an automatically expanding market, then you will not give much thought to how to expand it.' [17]

The resources were mainly geared to improving the efficiency of manufacturing their products.

2   There was the belief that there was no major substitute for products. This belief led to businesses focusing on improving their products rather than worrying about the substitutes. Most of the innovations came from outside the industry which, in many cases, provided salvation to the businesses.

3   Too much faith in mass production and declining unit production cost. In accordance with this belief, Levitt writes:

'All effort focuses on production. The result is that marketing gets neglected.'

In mass marketing what gets emphasised is selling and not marketing:

'Selling is preoccupied with the seller's need to convert his product into cash, marketing with the idea of satisfying the needs of the customer by means of the product and the whole cluster of things associated with creating, delivering and finally consuming it.' [18]

4   Some organisations believe that superior products will sell themselves. As a result, significant efforts are being made in the area of research and development. Such organisations are therefore, becoming increasingly product-oriented rather than market-oriented.

The author of this book remembers interviewing the production directors of a white goods industry in early 1970s. These directors believed marketing was a fad. They felt that the mission of organisations was to make superior products and to convince consumers to buy them. It was in the interest of consumers that efforts were directed towards improving products without taking into consideration consumer needs.

The consumers in the 1960s, according to Levitt, had 'stepchild status':

> 'They are recognised as existing, as having to take care of, but not worth very much real thought or dedicated attention.' [19]

In order to become market-oriented companies the following factors need to be considered:

- Organisations must consider and adapt to market conditions.

- Effective leadership has to consider the needs of customers.

- An organisation must view itself as a customer-satisfying organism.

- Every aspect of an organisation should be aware of its importance of customers.

- Gaining and retaining customers should be the primary consideration.

Source: *The above extracts are from 'Marketing Myopia'. Harvard Business Review, July-August, 1960. © 1960 by the President and Fellows of Harvard College: all rights reserved.*

Marketing Myopia was a landmark article because, for the first time, it made organisations realise that they were in a business of creating value for customers. It created a new mindset for strategists in considering the nature of business. The article created an impetus in thinking in marketing terms.

Today we talk about not just satisfying customers but delighting them. One ice cream company decided they were not in the business of making ice cream but delighting their customers (of all ages) by creating excitement for them.

One automotive company believed they were not in the business of making cars but manufacturing comfort and safety. Such 'marketing mindsets' came about because of the influence of gurus like Levitt.

Levitt wrote *"'Marketing Myopia' was not intended as analysis or even prescription; it was intended as manifesto."*

Many organisations jumped on the marketing bandwagon as a result of 'marketing mania'. Some had disastrous results because they did not understand Levitt's message.

Levitt's article also attracted a few critics. John Kay, writing in the Financial Times on 1 December 1995, argued that Levitt's thesis was fundamentally misconceived in that he confused evolution of an industry with the evolution of a market. He gives an example of washing machines and laundries being in the same market, because both are means of cleaning clothes. Washing machines and refrigerators are products of the same industry, despite their wholly different purposes, because each has a white box with a motor and is sold through similar distribution channels. In formulating corporate strategy industry is often confused with the market.

According to John Kay, to respond to the question 'what business are we in 'is to identify what are the distinctive skills and capabilities of the firm and ask what the markets are in which these yield competitive advantage.

Production Life Cycle

All marketing students should be conversant with the concept of Product Life Cycle. This concept describes a product's sales, profits, customers and competitors as having four stages: introduction, growth, maturity and decline.

Introduction

At this stage the product is first introduced to the market and efforts are being made for the product to gain a foothold in the market. Sales are likely to be slow and creep along slowly. At this stage competition is limited.

Initial customers are willing to take risks at this stage and they become innovators. Profit margins at this stage are very low and in some cases losses occur.

Growth

As the product acceptability gains ground, sales increase. This is the period when sales are rising at an increasing rate.

Maturity

As the product approaches the end of its growth stage, sales begin to decline. At this stage sales are still rising but at a decreasing rate. The product is thus said to pass the maturity stage.

Decline

After the maturity stage when most target customers own the product, the product enters this decline stage culminating eventually in its disappearance.

According to Levitt, at the **introduction stage** the demand for the product has to be 'created'. How long this cycle takes would depend on the nature of the product. Because of the uncertainties and the fatalities of many products at this stage, many organisations adopt what Levitt called *'used apple policy'*. They rather follow other organisations than become the pioneers. As he put it:

> *'The trouble with being a pioneer is that the pioneers get killed by the Indians'.*

At **growth stage** the rate of sales increase accelerates and the product takes off. Competitors enter the market and brand differentiation begins to develop. The marketing efforts are being directed towards consumers to prefer specific brands.

At **maturity stage**, market for the product becomes saturated. At this stage price competition becomes intense. The product is finely differentiated and more efforts are put on customer services.

At **declining stage**, few products weather the storm. Most of the producers, and with them their associated businesses, disappear from the market. Others form alliances and adopt various tactics to survive and the production gets concentrated into fewer hands.

Levitt urged managers to exploit the product life cycle. He felt the managers should try to foresee the profile of the proposed product's life cycle.

Even though in practice it would be difficult to foresee the precise nature of the life cycle and its duration, that should not mean no efforts should be made to use it effectively. It could be of great help to formulate new competitive moves.

He gives the examples of the companies which have successfully exploited product life cycles to consolidate their positions in the market place.

Understanding and taking into consideration the product life cycle would enable companies to adopt active rather than reactive product policy and come up with the ways to extend the life of the product at each stage.

Source: *Theodore Levitt. 'Exploit the Product Life Cycle'. Harvard Business Review, vol.43 (November-December, 1965). ©1965 by the President and Fellows of Harvard College: all rights reserved.*

Levitt popularised the concept of the product life cycle. Marketers should be interested in the product life cycle for the following reasons:

- They can assess the duration of the life cycles under different market conditions.
- They can be proactive in thinking about and coming up with the measures to extend the life of the product.
- They can plan their product investment strategies.
- They can anticipate changes in consumer buying behaviours.
- They can plan their product mix.

The duration and the pattern of the product life cycles vary depending on the nature of the product. A fad product would generally have a shorter life cycle than a traditional product.

The performance of each company in the industry at each stage of the product life cycle will depend on the marketing plan and marketing imagination of that company. A company that is very innovative and considers various marketing manoeuvres at each stage will perform better than a company that is mainly reactive.

Nariman Dhalla and Sonia Yuspeh in their article 'Forget the Product Life Cycle Concept'[20] have concluded from their study of four diverse products that:

- It is difficult to predict the stages of the life cycle;

- There are no clear-cut stages of the product life cycle

The life cycle is a useful tool but some experts believe it should not be used in forecasting.

It enables understanding of the marketing conditions and it keeps companies on their toes in addressing plans to compete effectively.

Differentiation

According to Levitt,[21]:

'There is no such a thing as a commodity. All goods and services are differentiable. Though the usual presumption is that this is truer of consumer goods than of industrial goods and services, the opposite is the actual case.

In order to examine various possibilities that exist in order to differentiate the product Levitt advises us first to understand the nature of the product itself.'

According to Levitt:

'Products are almost always combinations of the tangible and the intangible. An automobile is not simply a machine for movement visibly or measurably differentiated by design, size, colour, options, horsepower, or miles per gallon. It is also a complex symbol denoting status, taste, rank, achievement, aspiration, and (these days) being 'smart'- that is, buying fuel economy rather than display. But the customer buys even more than these attributes. The enormous efforts of the auto manufacturers to cut time between placement

and delivery of an order and to select, train, supervise, and motivate their dealerships suggest that these too are integral parts of the products people buy and are, therefore, ways by which products may be differentiated.' [22]

He classifies a product into 'The generic product' the thing itself; the expected product – things associated with the generic product such as delivery, terms, support efforts; the augmented product – attributes associated with the generic product beyond the customer expectations; the potential product – all the things associated with the product 'to attract and hold customers'.

'The way a company manages its marketing can be the most powerful form of differentiation... Brand management and product management are marketing tools that have demonstrable advantages over catchall, functional modes of management.'

'While differentiation is most readily apparent in branded, packaged consumer goods,, in the design, operating character, or composition of industrial goods, or in the features or 'service' intensity of intangible products, differentiation consists as powerfully in how one operates the business. In the way the marketing process is managed may reside the opportunity for many companies, especially those that offer generically undifferentiated products and services to escape the commodity trap.'

The globalisation of markets

Levitt wrote another trail blazing article in 1983 on the subject of globalisation. According to him there was a powerful force at play which was bringing the world together. That force was technology.

Technology has facilitated common tastes and common demands, thus 'homogenising markets everywhere'.

Technological advances have resulted in the creation of global markets and globally standardised products. Such global markets provide opportunity for organisations to reap economies of scale in production, distribution and marketing.

In economics there is a concept called 'demonstration effect'. According to this concept, there is a strong desire to emulate Western ways. Before World War II only a very few people in underdeveloped countries had much contact with the living standards of the Western World. All this began to change as American and European films began to be shown in numerous countries in the world. In addition to these films, magazines with photos and advertisements began to circulate widely and this created aspirations to live like westerners.

Finally, the development of air travel has enormously increased tourism to Latin America, Asia and Africa. Since the time when Levitt published his article technology (telephony, television) has made significant advances in linking countries together.

Homogenisation of the markets meant the end of multinational companies and the beginning of global companies. The differences between the two are as follows:

The multinational corporation operates in a number of countries taking into consideration local preferences and demand.

The global corporation operates as if the entire world is a single homogenised market. This means selling standard products everywhere and selling them in the same way. Such standardisation of products means achieving economies of scale and reduction of production costs. Such a strategy leads to achieving efficiency in production, distribution and marketing.

He writes:

> 'The multinational corporation knows a lot about a great many countries, and congenially adapts itself to their supposed differences. The global corporation knows one great thing about all countries, and lures them to its custom by capitalising on the one great thing they all have in common. The global corporation looks to the nations of the world not for how they are different but for how they are alike.'

He gives the examples of global successes achieved by organisations such as McDonalds, Coca-Cola, Pepsi, Sony, Levi and Revlon.

Globalisation of markets does not mean the end of choice or market segments. Levitt argued that the global phenomenon meant the beginning of price competition for quality products aimed at larger global segments. If one, for example, considers the acceptance of Indian food especially Indian curries in the United Kingdom (Curry, we are told has become number one 'English' food), it means that the curry market is aimed at much larger segment than a narrow ethnic market.

The globalisation process affects products and services, high tech as well as 'high-touch' products. What matters is producing such goods and services at high quality and selling them at low prices.

Levitt also argues that his globalisation thesis does not mean a disregard of national differences. As he writes:

> 'The difference between a distinction and a difference is that differences are perfectly consistent with fundamental underlying and surrounding sameness. Persistent differences can complement rather than simply oppose the advancement of commonalties – in society and business no less than in physics and space.'

Source: *The above extracts are from: Theodore Levitt: The Globalisation of markets'. Harvard Business Review, May-June, 1983. © 1983 by the President and Fellows of the Harvard College: all rights reserved.*

This was Professor Levitt's seminal article on Globalisation of markets. He anticipated the importance of technology in 'creating' global markets. Today, with the introduction of satellite dishes, global TV networks and the internet, the world is turning into a 'global village'.

Some writers give examples of organisations which followed Levitt's advice to globalise marketing and produce standardised products and services. These organisations including Parker Pen did not achieve success in global market.

According to some writers, organisations such as McDonalds and Coca-Cola which are quoted by Levitt in his article, succeeded because they introduced an element of localisation in their market and product mix. These organisations have followed 'global localisation' strategies as opposed to pure global strategy as advocated by Levitt. Global localisation means **'thinking globally and acting locally'**. Acting locally involves adapting sales promotion, distribution and customer service.

Different aspects of marketing mix are used by companies like Coca Cola, McDonalds, Unilever, and Gillette to gain a foothold in the global market. The particular approach an organisation adopts to global marketing will depend on its resources and distinct capabilities.

The standardised v. localised debate picked up tremendous momentum after the publication of Levitt's article. Numerous researches in the past decade suggest that the trend is toward the increased use of localised advertising.

The globalisation debate, triggered by Levitt has been extended to encompass global industry, global management and global competitiveness. The focus has been put on coordination, integration and configuration of value chains in order to inject flexibility of strategy and management at the heart of total global strategy.

Finally some writers argue that there are benefits to be gained by focusing on similarities in global customer needs as Levitt has suggested but it is also important to remember that advantages can also be gained by remaining responsive to differences in customer needs. Exploiting national differences can also develop into a source of competitive advantage.

At the feet of Theodore Levitt: Lessons learnt

- Do not focus on industry – focus on markets.

- Define your business in a broad and meaningful way.

- Define business in terms of consumer needs.

- Review your capabilities constantly to reflect changing market needs.

- There is no growth industry as such – only opportunities for growth.

- Create value for customers.

- Make use of product life cycle and come up with imaginative marketing solutions.

- There is no such a thing as a commodity.

- Differentiate by enhancing attributes associated with the generic product.

- Respond to the challenges of globalisation.

- Globalisation process affects products and services – tangibles and intangibles.

- Globalisation of markets does not mean the end of choice.

FOUR
Michael Porter

Michael Porter is a well known strategy guru. He is Harvard University's youngest tenured professor. Every strategy student can recite his 'Five Forces' model of competitiveness.

Porter built his reputation mainly by writing on strategy. All strategy students have to study Porter as a basic course requirement. His books include *'Competitive Strategy: Techniques for Analysing Industries and Competitors* (1980); *'Competitive Advantage: Creating and Sustaining superior Performance'* (1985); *'Competitive Advantage of Nations'* (1990); and numerous articles in the Harvard Business Review. His books adorn the shelves of Chief Executives, politicians, academics and business management students. He has been commissioned by the DTI and the Economic and Social Research Council to address the productivity gap as far as UK is concerned.

He has been appointed to a University Professorship, the highest professional distinction for a Harvard faculty member.

As a strategy guru he is included in this book because of his contribution on how firms compete and gain competitive advantage. Competition is a key aspect of marketing. According to Harvard University Gazette, his book *'Competitive Strategy: Techniques for Analysing Industries and Competitors'* is considered the pioneering treatise on corporate competition and strategy.

What does 'The Witch Doctors',[23] say about Michael Porter?

> 'Porter's work does not lend itself to one-line summaries, yet, under-
> neath all his lists and copious examples, there is arguably a fairly
> simple message. The essence of strategy is really about making a
> choice between two different ways of competing. One choice is
> market differentiation, competing on the basis of value added to
> customers, so that people will pay a premium to cover higher costs.
> The other choice is cost-based leadership, offering products or
> services at the lowest cost. Though quality and service is never
> irrelevant, reducing cost is the major focus of the second sort of
> organisation; and vice versa for the first. Porter's data showed that
> firms with a clear strategy performed better than those that either
> lacked a clear strategy or that consciously tried to follow both paths
> (i.e. lead the way in price and quality).'

Porter's Five Forces and marketing

Every student of strategy and marketing strategy should be conversant with Porter's five forces. In order to construct a competitive
strategy, an organisation needs to know what is likely to happen in
the markets in which the organisation delivers its products and services. It also has to know who its competitors are in a particular industry
structure.

Porter's Five Forces

In any industry the rules of the competition are governed by five
competitive forces. These are:

1   potential entrants,

2   competitive rivalry,

3   substitutes,

4   the bargaining power of buyers,

5   the bargaining power of suppliers.

These five forces address the question 'why are some markets more attractive than others?' The collective strength of these five competitive forces determines the ability of firms in an industry to earn, on average, rates of return on investment in excess of the cost of capital.

What constitutes these five forces?

1 POTENTIAL ENTRANTS

For potential entrants to any markets there are various barriers to overcome. These barriers arise due to economies of scale, product differentiation, capital requirements, and access to distribution channels, switching costs, government policies, experience, brand strength, and retaliation.

2 SUBSTITUTES

Direct and indirect substitutes. The more substitutes there are the less intense the competition will become.

3 COMPETITIVE RIVALRY

The strength and intensity of competition among the firms will depend on the number of firms operating in an industry sector. The factors which influence the competition are the number of firms and the key players, seller concentration, the relative size of the firms, market share, profitability, margins earned, added value, excess capacity available, and the strength of the brands.

4 BARGAINING POWER OF BUYERS

The factors include the demands for quality; playing off competitors; buyer concentration; are products a significant element in buyer costs? Buyers' price sensitivity; power of suppliers relative to buyers.

5 BARGAINING POWER OF SUPPLIERS

Few or many companies supplying customer firms; profitability of suppliers and capacity and utilisation; can suppliers integrate forward? High switching costs.

Using Porter's five forces framework, organisations can analyse and understand competition in a particular industry.

> 'All five forces jointly determine the intensity of industry competition and profitability, and the strongest force or forces are governing and becoming crucial from the point of view of strategy formulation. For example, even a company with a very strong market position in an industry where potential entrants are no threat will earn low returns if it faces a superior, low-cost substitute. Even with no substitutes and blocked entry, intense rivalry among existing competitors will limit potential returns...'

Source: *Porter, Michael. (1980) 'Competitive Strategy.'*

Marketing is about satisfying consumer needs. Private organisations would like to be effective in their marketing in order to make profits. Not-for-profit organisations would like to satisfy consumer needs in order to satisfy the mandate set for them either by government or sponsors.

Effective marketing depends on doing proper consumer research and also conducting industry and competitor analyses. This is why Porter's Five Forces framework becomes a useful tool in planning marketing strategy.

Apart from undertaking industry and competitive analysis, Porter also advises to focus on competitors. Organisations need to analyse who their key competitors are, what are their current strategies, what drives the competitors, what is their current profile, what capabilities they possess and what are their future intentions.

Pay attention to 'Market Signals.'

'A market signal is any action by a competitor that provides a direct or indirect indication of its intentions, motives and goals, or internal situation. The behaviour of competitors provides signals in a myriad of ways. Some signals are bluffs, some are warnings, and some are indirect means of communicating in the market place, and most if not all of a competitor's behaviour can carry information that can aid in competitors analysis and strategy formulation.'

Source: *Porter, Michael (1980). 'Competitive Strategy'.*

Doing intelligence work on competitors involves the systematic collection, collation, evaluation and use of intelligence about competitors.

How to conduct competitors' analysis

The following process reflects the five stages of conducting competitor analysis:

1 **Plan**. Decide what it is you are after.

2 **Collect**. Gather information on your key competitors. Information can be obtained from annual reports, investment analysis reports, company literature, competitor advertising, trade associations, customers, sales people and conferences.

3 **Process**. Process the information gathered.

4 **Evaluate**. Do detailed evaluation of information processes in terms of its reliability, appropriateness and usefulness.

5 **Communicate**. Communicate your findings to those who should know.

Strengths and weaknesses of conducting competitor analysis

STRENGTHS

- Companies are kept on their toes.

- Companies become aware of what competition is like and what their competitors are doing.

- Companies find out how their competitors are performing compared with their own performance.

- Helps the companies to refine and fine-tune their competitive strategy.

- It provides focus in relation to corporate strategy.

- Information can be used to conduct benchmarking in order to adopt best practice.

- The information reinforces marketing plan.

WEAKNESSES

- Some companies become bogged down by getting too much information and not doing anything with it. 'Too much analysis creates paralysis.

- Some get too involved in analysing information gathered to the extent that they do not spend enough time in their own businesses.

- Some undertake competitor analysis as a window-dressing exercise.

- Some collect very good information but do not follow it up with action plans and subsequent implementation.

Criticisms of Porter's Five Forces Framework

- Porter emphasised the need for a company to build a strategy in the context of the forces shaping its industry's profitability, while Gary Hamel and C. K. Prahalad (both leading strategy gurus – see Grundy's 'Gurus on Strategy') have emphasised instead the need for a company to identify its core competencies and build strategy around them.

- The framework is static in nature in a sense that it views industry structure as stable and externally determined.

- Differences in industry profitability do not necessarily determine the profitability of the organisation within them.

- It highlights competition at the expense of collaboration.

- Industry structure is also influenced by the dynamic nature of competition.

- The quality of strategic thinking in an organisation may be more important than industry structure in determining the overall performance of an organisation.

Porter's Value Chain and marketing

The value chain is the activities in which organisations engage in order to produce goods and services. This involves organisation's infrastructure, human resource management, technology, procurement, inbound logistics, operations, outbound logistics, marketing and sales and service. The concept of the value chain was made popular by Michael Porter in 1985 in his book *'Competitive Advantage: Creating and Sustaining Superior Performance'*.

Organisations aim to achieve optimisation of each element of the value chain. In analysing various elements, for example, inbound logistics (material handling, inspection, just-in-time delivery), outbound logistics (order processes, transport), marketing and sales (product development, pricing, promotion, distribution), service (on-site and off-site service, spare parts, customer care), organisations stand to gain insight not only into their own capabilities but also of their competitors' capabilities and competencies.

Porter distinguishes between primary activities and support activities. Primary activities are directly concerned with the creation of a delivery of a product or service. They can be grouped into the following areas: inbound logistics, operations, outbound logistics, marketing and sales and service. Support activities are there to improve effectiveness of primary activities. They consist of infrastructure, human resource management, technology development and procurement.

'A firm's value chain is embedded in a larger stream of activities that I term the value system. Suppliers have value chains (upstream value) that create and deliver the purchased inputs used in a firm's chain. Suppliers not only deliver a product but also can influence a firm's performance in many other ways. In addition, many products pass through the value chains of channels (channels value) on their way to the buyer. Channels perform additional activities that affect the buyer, as well as influence the firm's own activities. A firm's product eventually becomes part of the buyer's value chain. The ultimate basis for differentiation is a firm and its product's role

in the buyer's value chain, which determines buyer's needs. Gaining and sustaining competitive advantage depends on understanding not only a firm's value chain but how the firm fits in the overall value system.'

Source: *Porter, Michael. (1985). 'Competitive Advantage: Creating and Sustaining Superior Performance'.*

According to Grant[24]:

'Value chain analysis is most readily applicable to producer goods where the customer is also a company with an easily definable value chain and where linkages between the supplier's and the customer's value chains are readily apparent. However, the same analysis can be applied to consumer goods with very little modification. Few consumer goods are consumed directly; in most cases consumers are involved in a chain of activities before the total consumption of the product.

This is particularly evident for consumer durables. A washing machine is consumed over several years in the process of doing home laundry. The customer's value chain begins with search activity prior to purchase. In the home laundry process, the machine together with water, detergent, and electricity, is used to wash clothes, which are later dried and, possibly ironed. Continued use of the washing machine requires service and repair. We have complex value chains of manufacturer, retailer and consumer.

Even non-durables involve the consumer in a chain of activities. Consider a frozen TV dinner: it must be purchased, taken home, removed from the package, heated, and served before it is consumed. After eating, the consumer must clean any used dishes, cutlery, or other utensils. A value chain analysis by a frozen foods producer would identify ways in which the product could be formulated, packaged, and distributed to assist the consumer in performing this chain of activities.'

Value chains and their relevance to marketing

- They reflect organisational capabilities to undertake effective marketing.

- They can be used to analyse costs.

- They can be benchmarked against competitors' value chains.

- Market segments served affect the configuration of value chains.

- Outsourcing decisions can be made depending on the weaknesses of the value chain.

- They reinforce decisions to form strategic alliances and partnerships to enter new markets or gain specific capabilities to satisfy consumer needs.

- Value chains enable analysis of adding value to the customers.

Porter's generic strategies

In order to achieve an appropriate competitive positioning and above-average performance, Porter has proposed the following strategies which are termed as generic strategies:

Cost leadership

In this situation an organisation sets out to be the low-cost producer in its industry. It caters for many industry segments. If an organisation can achieve and sustain overall cost leadership then it will achieve superior performance. Cost leadership can be obtained by focusing on key accounts, reaping economies of scale, controlling costs.

A differentiation strategy

This strategy would involve an organisation in providing something unique to its target customers. The uniqueness can be related to products, the way it delivers its goods and services, the way it markets its products or anything that shapes a customer's perception in relation to differentiation. This could be the way products and services are branded or designed and the customers perceive such offerings as unique.

Focus strategy

This strategy involves an organisation being selective in terms of the segments it wants to serve and focusing on these segments to the exclusion of other segments. The focus strategy can either be cost focus or differentiation focus.

If an organisation does not choose generic strategies it wants to focus on then as Porter puts it, it will be *'stuck in the middle'*.

The extent to which a generic strategy can be sustainable will depend on competitors' behaviour and action. The organisation constantly has to be a step ahead of its competitors.

Generic strategies and marketing

Generic strategies affect the following elements of marketing:

- Costs and Pricing.
- Product design.
- Marketing mix.
- Channels of distribution.
- Promotion.
- Segmentation.
- Branding.

- Marketing information.

- Marketing communication.

- Profitability.

Differentiation and segmentation

According to Grant (1991):

> 'Differentiation is different from segmentation. Differentiation is concerned with how the firm competes – in what ways the firm can offer uniqueness to its customers. Such uniqueness might relate to consistency (McDonalds), reliability (Federal Express), status (American Express), quality (Marks & Spencer), and innovation (Sony). Segmentation, in terms of market segment choices is concerned with where the firm competes in terms of consumer groups, localities and product types.

> Whereas segmentation is a feature of market structure, differentiation is a strategic choice by a firm. A segmented market is one that can be partitioned according to the characteristics of customers and their demand. Differentiation is concerned with a firm's positioning within a market or a segment in relation to the product, service and image characteristics that influence customer choice...' [25]

Michael Porter also has addressed the issues of competitive advantage in relation to the nations. In his book 'The Competitive Advantage of Nations' (1990), Porter's view has an impact in relation to global competition and subsequently global marketing.

He puts forward a view that national conditions influence a firm's competitive advantage in internationally competing industries.

Factors which are likely to make a country attractive are summarised as follows:

Factor conditions

These factors relate to the resources a country possesses. They refer to the quality of physical and human resources, knowledge, capital and national infrastructure.

Porter's National Diamond

Demand conditions

The composition of home demand, the size and pattern of growth of home demand and the means by which the home demand influences products and services into foreign markets also determine national advantage in that industry. The conditions that provide incentive to invest and innovate will determine national competitive advantage.

Related and Supporting Industries

These are the industries and support services related to other industries which affect a particular industry in a country. These are what economists call 'external economies'.

If a country has internationally competitive and related industries they will be able to take advantage of one another's capabilities.

Firms Strategy, Structure and Rivalry

Differences in the way firms are managed and structured in a nation, the attitude towards risks, the way they compete, all these factors help to create a context within which industries operate.

Role of Chance

Some events such as wars, technological breakthroughs, unexpected changes in financial markets, and so on also play an important part in shaping a nation's competitive advantage.

The Role of Government

Governments can influence other key factors which determine national competitive advantage.

The above factors constitute what is known as 'Porter's Diamond'. Global marketing strategy should take account not only of the national diamond but also focus on the domestic diamond. It is the domestic rivalry that puts pressure on companies to look at global markets. Porter writes:

> 'And having been tested by fierce domestic competition, the stronger companies are well equipped to win abroad.'

> **Source:** *Porter, Michael (1990). 'The Competitive Advantage of Nations'.*

According to Warren Keegan[26]:

> 'Other researchers have challenged Porter's thesis that a firm's home-base country is the main source of core competencies and innovation. For example, Professor Alan Ragman of the University of Toronto argues that the success of companies based in small economies such as Canada and New Zealand stems from the diamonds found in a particular host country or countries. For example, a company based in a European Union (EU) nation may rely on the national diamond of one of the 14 other EU members. Similarly one impact of the North American free Trade Agreement (NAFTA) on Canadian firms is to make the US diamond relevant to competency creation. Rugman argues that, in such cases, the distinction between the home nation and host nation becomes blurred...'

Porter's key publications

- *'Competitive Strategy'* (1980). The Free Press.

- *'Competitive Advantage: Creating and Sustaining Superior Performance'* (1985). The Free Press.

- *'From Competitive Advantage to Corporate Strategy'*. Harvard Business Review. May-June, 1987.

- *'The Competitive Advantage of nations'* (1990). The Free Press.

- *'The Competitive Advantage of the Inner City'*. Harvard Business review. May-June, 1995.

- *'What is Strategy?'* Harvard Business Review. November-December, 1996.

- *'Competition'* (1998). Harvard Business Review Press.

- *'Can Japan Compete'* (2000).

- *'Strategy and the Internet'*. Harvard Business Review. March, 2001.

At the feet of Michael Porter: Lessons learnt

- Competition is an aspect of marketing.

- Strategy and competition are inter-related.

- Strategy formulation involves a choice.

- This choice involves differentiation, cost leadership and focus.

- The rules of competition are governed by five forces.

- Pay attention to the actions of competitors.

- Understand your value chain and conduct value chain analysis.

- Value chain reflects the organisation's capabilities.

- National conditions influence competitive advantage in internationally competitive industries.

- Domestic rivalries put pressure on companies to look at global markets.

FIVE
Philip Kotler

Kotler on marketing management

Philip Kotler is the world's pre-eminent marketing guru. He is S. C. Johnson and Son Distinguished Professor of International Marketing at the J. L. Kellogg Graduate School of management, Northwestern University.

He has published well over one hundred articles on marketing in the leading professional and academic journals and written various books on marketing including the most widely read book '*Marketing Management: Analysis, Planning, Implementation, and control*' published by Prentice Hall International Inc.

As a marketing guru and distinguished academic and writer he has popularised marketing as an academic subject.

In this chapter we will explore various concepts and theories which were presented in his widely recommended book '*Marketing Management: Analysis, Implementation, and Control*'. This book covers at great length key marketing concepts, advice on how these concepts can be applied, key marketing tools, macro and micro perspectives of becoming market-oriented companies. At micro level it covers at great length the subject of segmentation, consumer behaviour, market positioning, product development, managing product life cycles, designing pricing strategies and so on.

The attempt is made to explore briefly some of these topics in order to reflect the width of the subjects covered by Kotler in this well-publicised and widely-read book. **This book is a must for every marketing student and marketing practitioner.**

Importance and nature of marketing

Kotler argues that the economy has been radically transformed in the past two decades. This transformation has been brought about as a result of technological development and convergence and widening of geographical markets. Global marketing is expanding and various trade blocs are emerging to facilitate international trade.

Political dogmas are disappearing there is a great surge towards free market economies. The ways businesses do their marketing are changing to meet consumer needs.

At the social level there are significant demographic and societal changes which affect consumer lifestyles and their needs. Businesses need to respond to these changes.

According to Kotler the guiding principle now is customer value. Consumers rank products according to the value they generate. Marketers have to pay attention to the way consumers make decisions.

Marketing is based on the process of exchange. Exchange involves two parties and the process is influenced by value, cost and satisfaction. 'Exchange is the defining concept underlying marketing.'

For exchange to take place there have to be markets consisting of groups of people with specific needs for goods and services.

There are numerous markets in the modern economy. Manufacturers buy raw materials from 'resource markets', they use factors of production which they acquire from labour, capital and money markets and sell the finished products to customers and consumers.

Marketing therefore is a process of facilitating exchange. It is:

'a social and managerial process by which individuals and groups obtain what they need and want through creating, offering, and exchanging products of value with others.'

In order to achieve exchange, organisations have to plan, and implement the plan, to bring about exchange of goods and services. This is what marketing management is all about. It is:

'the process of planning and executing the conception, pricing, promotion, and distribution of goods and services, and ideas to create exchanges with target groups that satisfy customer and organisational objectives.'

Organisations conduct their marketing activity by:

1   Focusing on producing at high efficiency so as to sell their products and services at low price. Their marketing efforts will be directed towards these features.

2   Focusing on producing superior products that meet consumer needs. Their marketing efforts will be directed towards highlighting superiority of their products.

3   Focusing on selling. Such organisations believe that consumers have to be coaxed into buying products. Their resources, therefore, are used to promote selling. The aim is to sell what they make.

4   Focusing their attention on finding what customers want in relation to the target markets they are interested in and then delivering goods and services to these target markets more efficiently and effectively than their competitors. This way the organisations aim to satisfy their strategic objectives.

5   Focusing their attention to finding out and satisfying consumer and organisational needs but in addition they also plan to 'preserve or enhance the consumer's and the society's well-being.'

Marketing now affects profit as well as not-for-profit organisations and marketing management becomes important for all types of organisations.

Kotler then goes on to explore various concepts that constitute effective marketing management. He defines and explains the following concepts:

Customer value and satisfaction

Methods of tracking and measuring customer satisfaction include complaint and suggestion systems, customer satisfaction surveys, ghost shopping and lost customer analyses.

In explaining the concept of customer value he mentions the importance of value chain (popularised by Michael Porter, guru of strategy) as a company tool for identifying ways to create value for customers.

The value chain, as introduced by Michael Porter, involves the organisation's infrastructure, human resource management, technology, procurement, inbound logistics, operations, outbound logistics, marketing and sales and services.

Organisations aim to achieve optimisation of each element of the value chain. In analysing various elements, for example, inbound logistics (material handling, inspection, just-in-time delivery), operations (assembly, testing, processes, physical plant operations), outbound logistics (order processes, transport), marketing and sales (product development, pricing promotion, distribution) service (on-site and off-site, spare parts, customer care); organisations stand to gain insight not only into their own capabilities but also those of their competitors. Based on the analysis of the value chain they can prepare an effective marketing strategy for their goods and services.

Customer relationship

He also highlights the importance and the types of customer relationship. The **basic relationship** simply involves selling and buying and there is no further contact. The reactive relationship involves selling and buying but customers are encouraged to get in contact if more information is required or if there are complaints.

The **accountable relationship** involves selling and buying but the seller gets in touch with the customers after the purchase is made to find out if the customer is satisfied with the purchase.

The **proactive relationship** involves getting in touch with existing customers to inform of them of improvement made in the products.

Partnership relationship involves continuous contact with the customer with a view to bringing about customer savings.

Different organisations build and develop different types of relationship with their customers depending on the nature of the products and business.

In addition to customer relationship, Kotler also highlights the importance of customer retention by implementation of total quality.

'Ultimately', Kotler writes, 'marketing is the art of attracting and keeping profitable customers.'

Because of constantly changing marketing conditions successful organisations have to be ready to adapt. As a result organisations have to undertake strategic planning.

Strategic planning involves three key ideas. They are:

1   To manage 'a company's businesses as an investment portfolio for which it would be decided which business entities deserve to be built, maintained, phased down or terminated'

2   To assess accurately the future profit potential of each business by considering the market's growth rate and the company's position and fit.

3   For each business the company must develop a 'game plan'.

It is the responsibility of the corporate headquarters to formulate the whole planning process. Strategic planning involves setting strategic objectives according to the resources and capabilities of organisation. Setting processes and mechanism for implementation and monitoring and introducing flexibility to change the plan according to the changing macro-economic and social factors.

Kotler then introduces various analytical tools used by strategists. These tools are explained in detail by Tony Grundy in his book *'Gurus on Strategy'*, published by Thorogood and also in chapter ten of this book.

Marketing plan

The marketing plan should be developed in accordance with strategic plan. The organisation should articulate its mission and then formulate its strategy and strategic objectives. Resources should be planned and allocated to achieve these strategic objectives. From strategy should emerge corporate marketing strategy and marketing plan.... The market planning process involves analysing the following:

THE MARKET OPPORTUNITIES

Organisations have to analyse their strengths and weaknesses to find out how they can meet the challenges and take advantage of the opportunities which they face. Market research has to be undertaken to find out about consumer needs and wants and their purchasing behaviour. Research should focus on selected target marketing.

CONSUMER RESEARCH

Should provide answers on who are the customers? What do they buy? Why do they buy? What are they looking for in the products and services? How do they buy?

Based on the information gathered, organisations should then formulate their marketing strategies and prepare a marketing plan.

The marketing plan should pay particular attention to marketing mix – product, price, place and promotion.

Finally marketing plans have to be executed. Implementation of the plan has to be put in place and processes initiated to control and monitor the objectives set.

Kotler suggests three types of control. They are annual-plan control (the company is achieving its sales, profit and other targets), profitability control (measuring profitability of products) and strategic control (evaluating the marketing strategy and to ensure it is consistent with overall strategic planning).

Marketing information

Gathering information on products, customers, competitors and environment is very important function of a market-oriented organisation. An organisation needs to have a market information system to capture, analyse and act upon the information available.

What are the sources of information? They are:

- Sales records.
- Marketing intelligence.
- Marketing research.

Analysing the market environment

Macro perspective

Organisations operate within the context of external environment. Changes are constantly taking place at macro level and these changes pose threats as well as provide opportunities for the organisations.

Analysing what changes are taking place and how the organisation should respond to these changes become one of the key functions of a market-oriented organisation.

At macro level changes are taking place relating to demographic environment, economic environment, natural environment, technological environment, political environment and cultural environment. Changes within each category should be analysed and evaluated because they become the sources of threats and opportunities.

At consumer level it is important to find out the consumers' buying behaviour. This behaviour is affected by cultural factors, social factors, personal factors, and psychological factors.

From the information gathered, an organisation can ascertain the types of buying behaviour that exist and the processes consumers go through in order to arrive at buying decisions.

In addition, organisations should also try to understand the nature of the business market. Organisations deal with businesses in order to be able to provide goods and services. Business's behaviour and purchase decision-making needs to be understood in the same way as the consumers'.

Finally it is important to analyse the industry in which companies are involved and identify and analyse the company's competitors. Information should be gathered on who are the key competitors? What are their strategies? What are their strengths and weaknesses?

Micro perspective

Kotler then moves on to advising how to measure market demand, which market to measure and how to forecast demand. This information is important for managers in order that they fulfil their responsibilities.

Market segmentation

In order to target specific markets it becomes important to do market segmentation:

> 'Market consists of buyers, and buyers differ in one or more respects. They may differ in their wants, purchasing power, geographical locations, buying attitudes, and buying practices. Any of these variables can be used to segment a market.'

Segmentation procedure should be carried out periodically because market segments change. He then highlights the bases for segmenting consumer markets. These are geographic, demographic, and behavioural.

Market segments must exhibit five characteristics, namely, they must be:

1. **measurable,**

2. **substantial,**

3. **accessible,**

4. **differentiable** and

5. **actionable.**

In evaluating different market segments, a company must look at segment size and growth, segment structural attractiveness and company objectives and resources. Once the segments have been identified and evaluated a company can then consider its market positioning and its differentiation strategy.

'Differentiation allows the firm to get a price premium based on the extra value perceived by and delivered to the customers.'

Differentiation can be based on product, services, personnel and image. Differentiation should be effectively communicated to the segments concerned. Once the decision on differentiation is made a company can then position itself in the market place and prepare its competitive strategies.

Developing, testing and launching new products and services

It is important for companies to review their existing products and to develop new products to meeting changing market needs. There are dangers of new products failing if the best analytical tools and concepts are not applied properly or the company has not put in place an effective organisation for managing the new products.

According to Kotler the new product development process consists of the following stages:

- Idea generation.
- Idea screening.
- Concept development and testing.
- Marketing strategy development.
- Business analysis.
- Product development.
- Market testing.
- Commercialisation.

Team-oriented approach seems to be the best way some companies embark upon developing new products. Kotler then goes on to explain the way new product development should take place. He highlights various stages involved in innovation process and various techniques of product screening.

Product life cycle

Products have a limited life. They go through various stages from introduction stage to growth stage to maturity stage to decline stage. The product life cycle concept should be treated as a planning tool.

> 'The product life cycle portrays distinct stages in the sales history of a product. Corresponding to these stages are distinct opportunities and problems with respect to marketing strategy and profit potential. By identifying the stage that a product is in, or may be headed toward, companies can formulate better marketing plans.'

Kotler then goes on to detail various marketing strategies associated with each stage of product life cycle.

The rest of the book is devoted to designing marketing strategies for market leaders, challengers, Followers and Nichers; Designing strategies for the Global marketplace; Planning Marketing programmes and Organising, Implementing, and Controlling Marketing Effort.

What is a product?

One of the most popular marketing concepts Kotler puts forward is that of a product. He defines a product as anything that is offered to satisfy consumer need. In offering its product the marketer has to think in terms of five levels of a product. These are:

1 **Core benefits:** What benefits does the product offer.

2 **Generic product:** The overall product e.g. A car, a chair etc.

3 **Expected product:** What attributes buyers associate and expect from the product.

4 **Augmented product:** Additional services and benefits associated with the product.

5 **Potential product:** All that can be augmented in the future in relation to this product.

Such a concept provides opportunities to segment the market and deliver differentiation. (See similar views expressed by Theodore Levitt under differentiation, Chapter three).

Kotler then goes on to address managing service businesses and ancillary services. Services are intangibles, inseparable, variable and perishable. He goes on to show how marketers in the service sector can adopt and use marketing concepts.

In his book 'Marketing Professional Services' which he has co-authored with Paul N. Bloom,[27] he writes:

'The 1980s have become 'the Era of Marketing' in most of the professions. Marketing has helped to bring about a whole new competitive environment for professional service organisations. There are new types of firms offering new types of services in new types of locations. Fees are being billed in new ways and selling and advertising are being implemented using new, overt techniques.'

'The marketing of professional services is different, with several distinctive problems that must be confronted. Professional service organisations must deal with high levels of client uncertainty, limited product differentiability, quality control difficulties, and several other obstacles to mounting a successful marketing effort.'

Kotler's perspective on strategic marketing

Business activity takes place within the context of micro and macro environment. At macro level many factors influence business operations and business decisions. These factors are categorised as sociological, technological, economic and political.

At micro level the factors relate to the supply chain for the goods and services involving suppliers, distributors, partners and customers.

Businesses nowadays have to match their resources and competencies to achieve 'strategic fit'. Strategic fit and its environment change over time which makes the strategy formulation of any business a dynamic concept.

One way of responding to various changes is to consider the formation of 'Strategic Business Units (SBUs). According to Kotler, SBU has three characteristics. They are:

1   It is a single business or collection of related businesses that can be planned and separated from the rest of the company.

2   It has its own competitors.

3   Management of the SBU has control over most of the factors affecting profitability.

The SBUs should be given their own strategic planning goals and resources should be allocated to fulfil these goals. The role of the headquarters will be to review strategic planning goals of SBUs and to decide which of its SBUs to build, maintain, harvest and divest.

Kotler then explores various strategic analytical tools to explain how decisions are made. These tools include Boston Consulting Group Approach, General Electric Approach and, in relation to market entry for new businesses, Ansoff's approach.

Kotler's key publications

The range of the topics and issues covered by Philip Kotler is enormous and breath-taking. Following are some of his publications:

- Kotler, Phillip (2000) *'Marketing Management'*. Millennium edition. Prentice Hall.

- Kotler, Phillip (1999) *'Kotler on Marketing: How to create, win, and dominate markets.'* Free Press.

- Kotler, Phillip (1999) with Armstrong, Gary *'Principles of Marketing'* 8th edition. Prentice Hall.

- Kotler, Philip; Bowen, James; Makens, James C. (1998). *'Marketing for Hospitality and Tourism'* Prentice Hall.

- Kotler, Philip; Armstrong, Gary, *'Marketing: An Introduction.'* Prentice Hall.

- Kotler, Philip; Schiff, Joanne (1997). *'Standing Room Only: Strategies for marketing the performing arts.'*

- Kotler, Philip; Somkid Jatusripitak; Suvit Maesince (1997). *'The making of Nations. A strategic approach to building national wealth'* Free Press.

- Kotler, Philip; Stoller, Martin R. (1997). *'High Visibility: The making and marketing of professionals into celebrities.'* NTC Pub. Group.

- Kotler, Philip. (1996) *'Principles of Marketing'*. European edition. Prentice Hall.

- Kotler, Philip; Fox, Karen F. A. (1995). *'Strategic marketing for educational institutions'*.

- Kotler, Philip; Bloom, Paul N. (1984) *'Marketing Professional Services'*. Prentice Hall.

- Kotler, Philip (1982). *'Marketing for non-profit organisation'*. Prentice Hall.

At the feet of Philip Kotler:
Lessons learnt:

- The guiding principle in marketing is consumer value.

- Marketing is based on the process of exchange.

- This process incorporates socio-economic and managerial perspectives.

- Marketing affects all types of organisations – for-profit and not-for-profit organisations.

- To achieve success, organisations have to respond to changes in the external environment.

- Such responses necessitate preparation of a strategic plan.

- The strategic plan should be followed by marketing planning.

- The marketing plan should pay attention to marketing mix.

- Segment your market. Make sure the segments are substantial, measurable, accessible and actionable.

- Consider the nature of your product and service.

SIX
Tom Peters

In terms of 'guru' ranking Tom Peters must rank second to Peter Drucker. In terms of popularity he leads the conference platform. According to Charles Handy, himself a guru:

'Tom Peters is not a philosopher or a social historian like Peter Drucker. He no longer has any all-embracing theories of the world of organisations or any formulas for change but he gets under the skin of an organisation.'

The book *'The Witch Doctors'* [28] describes him in the following terms:

'...he has an intimate knowledge of corporate life, not just in the United States but also in Europe and around the Pacific rim; not just in the boardroom, but in the marketing department and in the machine shop; not just in the giants like Sony and IBM but in count-less small companies that nobody seems able to track down. He cannot book into a hotel, fly in an aircraft or park his car without finding an interesting management angle...'

Peter's first book, *'In Search of Excellence'* which he co-authored with his colleague Robert Waterman was a landmark book in that it was a launching pad for his way to become a business guru. The book looked at 43 successful companies and analysed the critical factors that contributed to their success. According to Peter Drucker, as quoted in *'The Witch Doctors'*:

'When Aunt Mary has to give that nephew of hers a high school graduation present and she gives him 'In Search of Excellence', you know that management has become part of the general culture.' [29]

They identified eight factors which contributed to excellence. **Getting close to Customers** was of one of these factors. Since then Peters has been emphasising the importance of customers and most of his seminars were focused on not just delivering to customers but delighting them.

The author of this book was privileged to 'stage 'Peters for nearly ten years when working at Management Centre Europe and then at the Economist Conferences.

The following extracts are from: Thomas J. Peters and Robert H. Waterman Jr. (1982) *In Search of Excellence: Lessons from America's Best-Run Companies.*

Close to the customer

'The customer is either ignored or considered a bloody nuisance.

The good news from the excellent companies is the extent to which, and the intensity with which, the customers intrude into every nook and cranny of the business – sales, manufacturing, research, accounting. A simple summary of what our research uncovered on the customer attribute is this: the excellent companies really are close to their customers. That's it. Other companies talk about it; the excellent companies do it.'

'In observing the excellent companies and specifically the way they interact with their customers, what we found most striking was the consistent presence of obsession.'

Peters and Waterman highlight the following service at their 'excellent' companies:

Service obsession

IBM, for example, answer every customer complaint within 24 hours; they really care about service; they are customer-driven and not technology-drive; they measure internal and external customer satisfaction on a monthly basis; they train their sales staff very effectively; they always act as if it were on the verge of losing every customer.

> 'In fact one of our most significant conclusions about the excellent companies is that, whether their basic business is metal bending, high technology or hamburgers, they have all defined themselves as service business.'

Quality obsession

The example provided is that of Caterpillar Tractor which:

> 'Offers customers forty-eight hour guaranteed parts delivery service anywhere in the world; that's how Cat is in first place ensuring that its machine works.'

Excellence of quality, reliability of performance and loyalty in dealer relationships seemed to be the guiding principles of the business.

chemanship

'The customer orientation is by definition a way of 'tailoring'- a way of finding a particular niche where you are better at something than anybody else. A very large share of the companies we looked at was superb at dividing their customer base into numerous segments so they can provide tailored products and service.'

'We find five fundamental attributes of those companies that are close to the customer through niche strategies:

1   astute technology manipulation

2   pricing skill

3   better segmenting

4   a problem-solving orientation and

5   a willingness to spend in order to discriminate.'

The strategies of all 'excellent' companies in various industrial sectors showed a bias towards value rather than cost.

Listening to the customers

'The excellent companies are better listeners. They get benefit from market closeness that for us was truly unexpected – unexpected, that is, until you think about it. Most of their real innovation comes from the market.'

Companies like Proctor and Gamble, Levi Strauss, have all come up with innovative products by collaborating with their customers.

Closing remarks: A controversy

'We should not close this chapter without mentioning briefly a major debate that has taken place within our own ranks. It is our belief, based on the excellent companies review, that the user is supreme as a generator and a tester of ideas. Several of our colleagues, on the other hand, maintain that companies are better driven by paying attention to technology and competitors. Moreover, Robert Hayes and William Abernethy, in a widely cited article in Harvard Business Review have attacked US companies for being too 'market-oriented' as opposed to 'technology oriented.' They argued that our short term focus has led us to be captive to the latest consumer preference polls.

We disagree.'

The 43 companies including IBM did not stay excellent for too long. IBM nearly disappeared. He later explains what had gone wrong but he passionately believed in customer orientation and went on to emphasise the importance of providing service excellence.

The following extracts come from: Tom Peters and Nancy Austin (1985). 'A Passion for Excellence: The Leadership Difference', Random House.

In this book Peters and Austin emphasise the importance of 'care of customers', 'constant innovation', and 'people' and the centre of these is leadership. They write:

'Obsessive pursuit of the customer and constant innovation mean adaptation. To pursue the customer and to pursue innovation, are to be in constant commerce with the outside world, listening and thus adapting.'

In chapter 8 they spell out:

'Twenty two aspects of a true customers-first orientation. Almost all are missing from most management and even marketing texts. The list is not meant to be exhaustive...'

The following extracts come from: Tom Peters (1987). *'Thriving on Chaos'*, Alfred A. Knopf.

There are no excellent companies as the world is changing fast and companies have to be flexible. Hence the title of his book *'Thriving on Chaos'*. However, he again revisits many of the issues relating to customers and here are some of the highlights:

- Only those who pay attention to customers and 'become attached to customers will survive.

- Companies must create and add value to every product and service.

- Companies must constantly create new market niches.

He quotes Regis McKenna,[30] Silicon Valley marketing expert. McKenna's view constitutes what Peters believes should happen in order to thrive on chaos.... Mckenna writes:

> *'Marketing should focus on market creation, not market sharing. Most people in marketing have what I call 'market-share mentality'. They identify established markets then try to figure a way to get a piece of a market... All these strategies are aimed at winning market share from other companies in the industry.*

> *In fast-changing industries, however, marketers need a new approach. Rather than thinking about sharing markets, they need to think about creating markets. Rather than taking a bigger slice of the pie, they must try to create a bigger pie. Or better yet, they should bake a new pie.*

> *Market-sharing and market- creating strategies require very different sorts of thinking. Market-share strategies emphasise advertising, promotion, pricing and distribution. The supplier with the best financial resources is likely to win.*

> *Market- creating strategies are much different. In these strategies, managers think like entrepreneurs. They are challenged to create new ideas.*

The emphasis is on applying technology, educating the market, developing the industry infrastructure and creating new standards. The company with the greatest innovation and creativity is likely to win.

... If companies think only about sharing the markets, they will never get involved in emerging businesses. They will take a look at the business decide that the 'pie' is too small, and move on to other possibilities.

This is exactly what happened in the personal-computer business. Dozens of major companies investigated the market for inexpensive computers in the mid-1970s. At the time, these computers were used primarily by hobbyists – that is, enthusiasts who enjoyed tinkering with the machines...

But a few companies such as Apple and Tandy, looked at the business with a market-creation mentality. They looked beyond the hobbyists and saw that small businessmen and professionals might eventually use the machines – if only the machines were designed and marketed a bit differently. Rather than focusing on what was they focused on what might be.'

Peter's on marketing and marketing issues

The themes covered in 'Thriving On Chaos' include 'creating niches' and 'differentiating commodities'; providing quality as perceived by the customer; providing superior service; achieving total customer responsiveness; becoming obsessed with listening to customers; turning manufacturing into a marketing weapon; making sales and service forces into heroes.

Customers and marketing occupy half his book. Marketing issues include **differentiation** – he makes the point that:

> '... differentiation only happens when the customer understands the difference'; **quality** as perceived by customers; providing **service excellence** – 'Consider every customer to be a potential lifelong customer.' and 'Attend especially to the **intangible attributes of the product and service**; achieve total customer responsiveness and create a **partnership relationship** with suppliers' – 'Adversarial relations with suppliers, distributors (and all members of the distribution channel), and ultimate end users must be quickly replaced with partnership relations.'; adopt an **international** perspective – examine joint ventures and alliance opportunities; stand out from the growing crowd of **competitors**; **listen to your customers** and those who are at the coalface; integrate manufacturing with marketing – 'make manufacturing or operations a – or the – prime marketing tool.' Focus on **sales** staff and sales training.

The rest of the book is adapted to 'enablers', the things companies must do, such as management style and structure, to achieve superior performance.

In my view this book is 'a must read' for marketing students and marketing practitioners.

The customer theme is incorporated on his next book 'The Pursuit of WOW!'

The pursuit of WOW!

- Every job has customers. Have every employee identify who his or her customers are.

- Have all top corporate/divisional managers pledge two days per month to customer visits (puny, really), two days per month to supplier and distributor visits.

- Make sure that every person in the organisation makes at least two customer visits a year.

- Make the words glow, tingle, thrill, dazzle, delight – and, of course, WOW – the primary bases for evaluating the quality of all your products and services; i.e. do customers like your service (bad), or are they 'gaga' over it (good, great, fantastic!)?

- Each year have customers systematically evaluate every one of your quality and service measures.

- The 10 senior members of your corporate management: At the next industry trade show, demonstrate the most sophisticated product your outfit makes.

- Finance and accounting staff: Spend at least two days per week in the 'field' with internal customers (half your performance appraisal should be based on evaluations designed and executed by customers).

Source: *Tom Peters (1994). 'The Pursuit of WOW!' Macmillan*

Service with soul

> 'There are 50 ways to leave your lover, but only six exits from the airplane...'
>
> START OF THE SAFETY ANNOUNCEMENT SOUTHWEST AIRLINES
>
> 'Southwest Airlines is so far ahead of the competition it hardly seems fair...'

While Kelleher gives his customers a great deal and a great time, he's clear that people of Southwest come first – even if it means dismissing customers! Are customers always right? 'No, they are not', Kelleher snaps. 'I think that's one of the biggest betrayals of your people you can possibly commit. The customer is frequently wrong. We don't carry those sorts of customers. We write them and say, 'Fly somebody else. Don't abuse our people.'

Want to increase customer-service consciousness? Forget banking orders. Or issuing a 'Customers First' vision statement (plasticised, of course). Instead:

- Prominently post customer-service statistics all over the place.

- Distribute all good and bad customer letters to everyone. (Do mark over any offending employee's names in the letter – public humiliation is hardly the point.)

- Plaster pictures of customers (buyers, products, facilities, etc.) all over the walls.

- Invite customers to visit any facility, any time; urge salespeople to bring customers through the plant, distribution centre, accounting office.

- Start making weekly awards for 'little' acts of customer heroism.

- Use customer-service story (good or bad – 90 per cent good) as the lead story in every company / department newsletter.

- Hold an all-hands, half hour 'wins and losses' meeting on new orders and lost orders every Thursday at 8am.

70 per cent of lost customers hit the road not because of price or quality issues but because they didn't like the human side of doing business with the prior provider of the product or service.

In the age of e-mail, supercomputer power on the desktop, the internet, and the raucous global village, attentiveness – a token of human kindness – is the greatest gift we can give someone: any one including our American or Japanese or German customers for paper clips, ham and cheese sandwiches, jet aircraft engines or $10 million lines of credit.'

The following extracts come from: Tom Peters (1994), '*Tom Peters Seminar*', Vintage Books.

In this book Tom Peters gives example after example to reinforce his message of getting close to customers.

'The Associated Group broke itself into itty-bitty businesses, the Acordia companies that would have no choice but to schmooze and become intently, intimately, and emotionally involved with micro bits of the financial -services marketplace.

Body Shop founder Anita Roddick refuses to spend a dime on conventional advertising. Instead, she works with her shops to create ongoing 'conversations' between staff and customers. She wants the Body Shop to be a teaching institution, not just another cosmetics peddler.

The premier German machine-tool maker Trumpf, plays by similar (self-invented) rules: It is a teaching institution, working hard with customers so that they can clearly understand how to benefit from Trumpf's enormous and unequalled technical skills (which come accompanied by a higher sticker price).'

He goes on to give example of Nypros of Clinton, Massachusetts (purveyor of injection-moulded plastic parts). It provides materials used to produce lenses to Vista on, the Johnson & Johnson unit. Nypros and Vistakon work together to assess production processes, quality and productivity. The two organisations are linked together by computers and collaborate openly and honestly.

Nypros have similar collaborative arrangements with Gillette.

'We really mean it when we talk about satisfying customers, because that's all we have. We don't have any 'products', says Nypro CEO Gordon Lankton.

The following extracts come from: Tom Peters (1992) 'Liberation Management: Necessary Disorganisation for the Nanosecond Nineties.'

As the title suggests the theme of this book is about managing in turbulent times. He advises on how to manage when the key drivers of change – globalisation and technology – are transforming the business landscape.

He, however, revisits his consistent theme on taking customers seriously. In chapter 47, he writes:

'Look through clear eyes and you'll find that all enterprises – hospitals, manufacturers, banks – are organised around and for the convenience of, the 'production function.' The hospital is chiefly concocted to support doctors, surgery and lab work. Manufacturers are fashioned to maximise factory efficiency. The bank's scheme is largely the by-product of 'best backroom (operations) practice.' I am not arguing there's no benefit to customers from these prac-

tices. The patient generally gets well, the car or zipper usually works, and the bank account is services. And enterprises do reach out, sporadically, to customers – holding focus groups, providing toll-free numbers to enhance customer dialogue, offering 'customer care' training to staff. But how many build the entire logic of the firm around the flow of the customer through the A to Z process of experiencing the organisation? Answer: darn few!'

'Such 'outside-in' imagery clashes with the current 'customer focus' craze. Customer focus still clutches the tired imagery of 'us' designing to attend to 'them'; 'us' as active (the actors); 'they' as passive (audience); 'us' as the sun around which 'they' the customers revolve. In an illusory world, semantics by definition are everything – and 'outside-in', 'script-and-direction-by-customer,' or 'customer-experience created' are more appropriate phrases. 'We'(producers) are mere derivative, the bit players in 'their'(customers) show, not the reverse!

I have come to call all this 'customer zing'. It's an ugly word. And in general I heartily dislike such concoctions. Yet it seems to taste about right. One reason for choosing it is to point up the difference from customizing. Customizing, a good idea, is still pre-Copernican in slant. 'We' are still the centre of the universe, presenting 'them with a carefully crafted menu of offerings. It misses that huge Disney-leap into their creating us. Customer-as-initiator is the point.'

He presents the following traits of the totally customerised company:

- Personalisation.
- Customisation.
- Responsiveness.
- Friendliness.
- The perception of choice.
- Insiderism.

- Clubbishness.

- Transparancy.

- In the know.

- House calls.

- Design that suits my convenience.

- Human scale.

- An educational experience.

- Reliability.

- Fun.

- Theatre.

- Emphasis on beginning and ends.

- Consistency.

- Class.

- Emphasis on process.

- Caring – a must.

The following extracts come from: Tom Peters (1997) '*The Circle of Innovation*' Alfred A. Knopf.

The book focuses on the importance of innovation for any business today in order to survive in a changing business climate. Yet again he is loyal to his theme and his passion – the customers.

On the theme of empowering customers he writes:

> *Empowerment (customers) = Information = access = decision making = choice = customisation = perception of control/ownership.*

He gives numerous examples of organisations including Netscape, Charles Schwab, and his personal experience of empowering customers.

Peter's key publications

- Peters and Waterman Jr. *'In Search of Excellence: Lessons from America's Best-Run Companies.'* (1982). Harper and Row.

- Peters, Tom: *'Liberation management: Necessary Disorganisation For the Nanosecond Nineties.'* (1992) Macmillan.

- Peters, Tom: *'The Pursuit of Wow!'*(1992). Vintage Books.

- Peters, Tom. *'Thriving on Chaos'* (1987). Alfred A. Knopf.

At the feet of Tom Peters: Lessons learnt

- Get close to your customers.

- Focus on service excellence.

- Listen to your customers.

- Innovate constantly.

- Create niches and differentiation.

- Consider every customer to be a potential life-long customer.

- Be customer-led and not production-led organisation.

- Empower your staff.

- Empower your customers.

- Do not satisfy your customers but delight them.

SEVEN
George Day

George day is Geoffrey T. Boisi Professor of Marketing at Wharton, University Of Pennsylvania. He has won various awards for his work and publications in marketing and he consults widely to business and government on marketing management and competitive strategies.

He has held visiting professorships at Sloan School of Management, Massachusetts Institute of Technology, Graduate School of Business, Harvard University, and London Business School.

Day on strategic marketing planning

In his book *'Strategic Marketing Planning: the Pursuit of Competitive Advantage'* (1984), Professor Day presents the following perspectives:

- Strategy is important for any organisation as it presents the direction the organisation would like to pursue to achieve its objectives. It also serves as an integrating factor which co-ordinates various departmental and divisional objectives.

- Changes in the external environment have put pressure on organisations to be proactive rather than reactive in formulating their strategies. He writes, 'The primary responsibility of strategic planning is to look continuously outward and keep the business in step with the anticipated environment. The lead role in meeting this responsibility is played by marketing, for this is the boundary function between the firm and its customers, distributors and competitors.

'...Marketing embraces the interpretations of the environment and the crucial choices of customers to serve, competitors to challenge, and the product characteristics with which the business will compete.'

- In strategy formulation there are generally two types of approach. The first one is 'outside-in' approach where the firm assesses the external environment and tries to respond to changes by coming up with strategic options. Then there is 'inside-out' approach where the firm assesses its resources and capabilities and then formulates its strategies to meet the challenges of changing external environment. Professor Day proposes the third approach 'the strategic thinking approach' which integrates both outside-in and inside-out approaches.

- Various methods including market segmentation, product life-cycle analysis, and portfolio analysis are used in strategic planning practice. He then explores various stages involved in the evolution of strategic planning.

Professor Day also believes that it is important to define the nature of business; the point made by Peter Drucker and Theodore Levitt. Definition of business should assume multi-dimensional perspectives involving customer functions, technology development, segmentation, and value-adding system.

Day then provides what he calls 'an anatomy of Competitive Strategies' and focuses on cost cutting, differentiation, and serving a protected niche market. Differentiation would only work if they:

'can be converted into:

1 *benefits,*

2 *perceived by a sizeable group,*

3 *what these customers value and are willing to pay for, and*

4 *cannot readily obtain elsewhere.'*

These strategies are similar to Porter's generic strategies highlighted in his book 'Competitive Strategy'.

The distinctive features of strategic Market Planning Process should involve:

- Conducting environmental scanning;

- Competitor analysis,

- Assessing resources and competencies and going through SWOT (strengths, weaknesses, opportunities and threats) analysis.

Day integrates market focus with competencies focus in the planning process. In terms of analysing the markets Day explains bottom-up approach (starting from customers) and top-down approach. In formulating various strategic options Day advocates adoption of creative thinking. Finally he focuses on implementation.

His contribution on market-driven strategy

George Day is said to be a pioneer in putting a market focus at the centre of the strategy process. According to 'marketing Wharton':

> 'Today, virtually every company talks about focusing on the market but few are truly successful in realising this vision. To become market driven, companies need to do more than rethink their strategies; they need to rebuild their organisations. In research and work with hundreds of executives in diverse industries, Day has identified some of the distinguishing characteristics of market driven organisations and strategies for building them. He sums up these insights in his new book, **'The Market-Driven Organisation'** (1999) published by Free Press.'

An interview with George Day:

The following interview with George day provides key insights of his view on what is meant to be 'market-driven'.

KNOWLEDGE @ WHARTON

How has the view of being 'market-driven' changed in the past decade?

DAY

For more than 40 years, firms have been exhorted to listen to their customers and make decisions from the market back. Only in the past decade has this article of faith become a corporate priority for most firms as they recognise the performance benefits of being market driven. We have also learned that a customer focus is an essential condition but not a sufficient guide to action. The only way a business can succeed is to deliver superior customer value, and that requires an intense emphasis on competitors who set the performance standard. Advances in information technology also are bringing us closer to the ideal of an organisation that is continually responsive to the changing requirements of customers.

KNOWLEDGE@ WHARTON

You write in your book that while market-driven rhetoric is now commonplace, successful market-driven organisations still are rare. Why?

DAY

There is still some confusion about what it means to be market-driven. But I think the most important reason why the desire to be market-driven is not translated into action is the organisation itself. In my work with senior executives, I found one of the greatest stumbling blocks to implementing a market-driven strategy was that their organisations were not suited to the task. One 3M manager summed up the problem this way: 'The fact that we are a multi-dimensional, multi-functional, multi-regional, multi-plant organisation is not the customer's fault.'

You cannot take an internally focused, bureaucratic organisation and suddenly expect to be tightly linked to the market. It's like taking a military regiment and expecting the soldiers to suddenly become sprinters. It just won't happen without some reconditioning. It requires a rethinking of the entire organisation, building new capabilities. It was the ability to make these deeper changes that separates the firms that talk about becoming market-driven from those that are doing so successfully.

KNOWLEDGE@WHARTON

What does it mean to be market-driven?

DAY

Market-driven organisations have superior skills in understanding, attracting and keeping valuable customers. These skills allow companies to keep their strategy aligned with changing market requirements. Even firms with world-class technology and innovative business models have to stay close to their customers and ahead of competition to realise their full potential. Market-driven organisations have an externally oriented culture, capabilities for market sensing and market relating, and a configuration that aligns vertical functions and horizontal processes. All of these elements work together to foster a market orientation.

KNOWLEDGE@WHARTON

Why is it important to be market-driven?

DAY

While many competitive advantages are rapidly eroded in today's environment, connections to customers are more dynamic and enduring if they are well developed and maintained. These links to the market can help company's weather changes in the environment and anticipate these changes to outperform rivals in finding ways to provide value to customers. For example, Intuit used superior capabilities in market sensing and relating to gain a near monopoly in personal finance software despite fierce competition from dozens of competitors – including Microsoft, which had bested rivals in word processing, spreadsheets and presentations. Intuit managed not only to survive but to dominate.

The company worked closely with customers to make its Quicken soft-ware, a financial planning programme, easier to use. Teams of software developers watched for small hints of where the programme might be difficult or confusing, worked in usability labs and even visited customers at home to identify problems and improve the software. In this process, they identified and filled a need for small business accounting software, and Quick Books went on to capture 70 per cent of the market within two years of introduction.

KNOWLEDGE@WHARTON

You said there is some confusion about the concept of being market-driven. What is being misunderstood?

DAY

There are three common pitfalls. Some companies become so product-focused that they become 'oblivious to the market'. Recognising the weakness of this internal focus, other companies become 'customer-compelled,' bending over backward to do whatever customers want. This leads to diluted and uncoordinated efforts. It also ultimately leads to the third pitfall, which is to feel superior to the market. After seeing the weaknesses of following customers, some managers advocate 'ignoring the customer'. If customers can't tell you what they want, managers figure they should just ignore them. But the idea of ignoring the customer is just as dangerous as slavishly following them.

KNOWLEDGE@WHARTON

How can it be dangerous to follow customers?

DAY

Customers sometimes can't tell you what they want. For example, when Ford asked customers if they wanted a second sliding door on the Wind Star in 1995, they didn't appear to be interested. So Ford, as a customer-focused (or, perhaps customer-compelled) company, took them at their word. Chrysler looked a little deeper and correctly anticipated that customers would want the extra door. Chrysler was right and it cost Ford $560 million to rectify the mistake.

Isn't Ford's mistake – and the successes of products that no customer asked for, like the Walkman and Chrysler's minivan – an argument for ignoring customers?

DAY

That is unfortunately the lesson many managers draw from such experiences. Executives have many more sophisticated ways to identify customer needs or desired attributes rather than getting their feedback on specific products. While customers can't always tell you what they want, they usually can show you what they need. In the early 1970s, for example, no customers were asking for fax machines but Xerox identified a demand for one million units by looking at the extent and frequency of urgent written messages (Unfortunately, it chose a computer-to-computer technology – a solution that proved to be a couple of decades ahead of its time.) Between the two extremes of being compelled by customers and ignoring the customer is the profitable middle ground of a balanced customer-focus.

KNOWLEDGE@WHARTON

Which companies do you feel are doing this well?

DAY

Different companies have excelled at solving different pieces of puzzle. The power of a market driven organisation also can be seen in the success of companies such as Wal-mart, Virgin Airlines, Disney, Gillette, and many others that have used a superior relationship to customers to gain advantage over rivals. In contrast, the stories of IBM's loss of control of the PC market, Motorola's stumble in shifting from analogue to digital cellular systems, and Sear's difficulties in the early 1990s, show how a failure to align the organisation to the market can quickly and seriously erode competitive advantage.'

December 10, 1999. © Wharton School of the University of Pennsylvania

The following extracts come from Marketing Wharton.

Why do some companies succeed at customer relationship management (and many fail)?

It's a question that formed the basis of a survey that George Day sent to senior managers in 342 medium-to-large-sized businesses from the manufacturing, transportation, public utilities, wholesale and retail trade, finance, insurance and real estate sectors. Day also conducted in-depth interviews with managers at 14 companies within the 342-firm sample, including Dow Chemical, Verizon Information Systems, GE Aircraft Engines and Ford.'

The results suggest there are three different approaches to customer relationship management (CRM), each with dramatically different results.

Market-driven approach

This approach makes CRM a core element of a strategy that focuses on delivering superior customer value through such elements as exceptional service and a willingness to cater to individual requirements.

Day cites Fidelity Investment's decision to invest in understanding and segmenting its customers as an example. In 1997, the company switched from a 'product-centred orientation', which meant pushing only their own funds and treating all customers the same way, toward a relational orientation based on tailored education and investment recommendations. This included such things as expanding their offerings to include non-Fidelity funds and presenting investment recommendations tailored to each investor's needs.

What made the strategy come alive was Fidelity's ability to vary the value proposition in systematic ways within each of 17 customer segments, which in turn were based on four larger customer groupings. These included the high value segment (with large complex portfolios that needed hand-holding); core customers (interested in investing but not actively involved in it); active traders (interested in top-notch execution of their trades); and institutions and small businesses offering retirement plans for employees.

Inner-directed approach

These initiatives are aimed at better organising internal data to cut service costs, help sales staff close deals faster and better target marketing activities – tasks that are usually assigned to the information technology group and have little connection with competitive strategy.

CRM technology is frequently a focus of this approach, and indeed, CRM software programmes remain the fastest growing area in customer management. Day contends that CRM technology has been oversold, noting recent studies suggesting that close to 20 per cent of CRM initiatives actually make things worse.

The odds of disappointment with the inner-directed approach are high because the primary motivation is to solve the company's problems, not to offer better value to customers.

Defensive actions approach

This approach includes loyalty programmes based on redeeming points in a frequent-flyer or frequent-buyer programme – designed to deny an advantage to a competitor. While there is little chance of gaining an advantage, this type of approach at least maintains the status quo.

Day's conclusions

Superior performance comes from integrating three components of the customer-relating capability: an organisational **orientation** that makes customer retention a priority and gives employees wider latitude to satisfy customers, **information** about relationships, including the quality of relevant customer data and the systems for sharing this information across the firm; and **configuration** – the alignment of the organisation toward building customer relationships, achieved through incentives, metrics, organisational structure and accountabilities.

He was surprised to find out that what separates the good firms from the bad is their configuration.

Yet in looking at the 18 per cent of the sample that are the relationship leaders, what sets them apart is their orientation. The emphasis all throughout these companies is on customer retention. Everybody is concerned about it, not just the marketing group or the sales group.

His conclusions also hold up in all types of markets, whether B2B or B2C.

The 'Red Queen' syndrome

Orientation perspective

Day cites IBM under CEO Lou Gerstner for insisting the company takes only the best customers – and then does everything possible to cater to their needs. This approach saved IBM from the problems facing companies like H-P, Cisco and Compaq which chased every internet start-up without regard to their long-term ability to pay.

Configuration perspective

Day found out that very few companies emphasised customer satisfaction and retention in their incentives. Siebel Systems, the leader in CRM software, is obsessively focused on customer satisfaction tying 50 per cent of management's incentive compensation and 25 per cent of salespeople's compensation to measures of customer satisfaction.

Superior configurations also have organisation structures that ensure the customer has a seamless interaction with the company.

Information perspective

This perspective is less important than orientation and configuration in distinguishing leaders from followers. Most companies were investing in data mining, databases and software because this was the easy thing to do in benchmarking against competitors.

Day concludes that big investments in CRM technology are yielding negligible competitive advantages. It is the classic 'Red Queen' syndrome; although they are running faster and faster they stay in the same place.

One of the reasons many CRM failures occur is because companies concentrate on the customer contact processes without making corresponding changes in internal structures and systems.

Before focusing on customer retention which is very important, it is necessary to know why customers are defecting. Is defection due to poor service poor delivery, poor quality, or are customers polygamous i.e. used to shopping around.

He also makes the point that successful relationship managers are always collaborating in their successes against their competitors. In the sophisticated financial services industry, for example, Fidelity, Schwab and Merrill are all highly competent. But Fidelity and Schwab have an edge... because of their orientation.

Note: George Day states that nobody before has looked at whether being a relationship leader gives companies a competitive advantage, and by extension, significantly influences their profitability.

Companies that make relationship management a central part of their strategy are going to be the ones that win.

He examines in detail the strategies of two credit companies, Capital One and First USA and shows how different approaches to customer data and customer responsiveness have led Capital One to consistently outperform First USA.

Firms that sustain their commitment along the lines George Day has highlighted send a signal to both employees and customers that their customer-relating capability is one of the centrepieces of their strategy.

Source: *Adapted from Marketing Wharton, published in January, 2003.*

The results of Day's surveys and interviews appear in his latest research paper entitled 'Winning the Competition for Customer Relationship' which will appear in the Sloan Management Review in spring, 2003.

Day's key publications

- *'Strategic Market Planning: The Pursuit of Competitive Advantage'*. (1989), West Publishing.

- *'Market-Driven Strategy: Processes for Creating value'* (1990), Free Press

- *'The Market-Driven Organisation: Understanding, Attracting and Keeping Valuable Customers'* (1999). The Free Press.

- *'Strategies for Surviving a Shakeout'*, Harvard Business Review, March-April, 1997.

He has published extensively in various professional and academic journals and has co-authored numerous books on marketing.

He is not as well-known as Levitt or Kotler but he is very highly regarded by business executives and students. At Management Centre Europe in Brussels, he was among the key marketing gurus that I had the privilege to stage and hear his presentations.

At the feet of George Day: Lessons learnt

- Be proactive not reactive.

- Marketing should play a leading role.

- Approaches to assessing external changes should be integrated.

- Definition of business should assume multi-dimensional perspectives.

- Integrate marketing focus with competencies focus.

- Advances in information technology enable organisations to be responsive to external changes.

- To be market-driven, acquire skills in understanding, attracting and retaining customers.

- Do not become 'oblivious to the market'.

- Do not bend over backwards to do what customers want.

- Do not at the same time ignore your customers.

EIGHT
Jagdish Sheth

Dr. Jagdish Sheth is Professor of Marketing at the Goizueta Business School, Emory University. He is nationally and internationally known for his scholarly contribution in marketing, customer behaviour, global competition and strategic thinking.

He has published more than 200 books and research papers representing different areas of marketing. His book with John Howard 'The Theory of Buying Behaviour' (1969) is a classic in the field.

His publications include topics and themes relating to customer behaviour, telecommunications management, global macroeconomic perspectives, research in marketing, marketing theory, export marketing.

His latest books 'The Rule of Three: What It Is and How It Works' (2003, The Free Press) presents a theory of market evolution. This is a ground breaking theory in the area of global competition. This book provides information to those who seek to forecast trends and develop strategies that result in success.

The range of subjects covered by Professor Sheth is breath-taking. The following information provides some insight into his influence in the field of marketing including developing client relationships.

The following extract comes from: Eds: Philip Kotler and Keith K. Cox (1988) *'Marketing Management and Strategy: A Reader'*, Prentice Hall:

> *'Professor Jagdish Sheth has made a mark in the area of organisational buying behaviour. In marketing, emphasis is paid on consumer behaviour at individual level. Sheth came up with a model to explain how decisions are made collectively at organisational level'.*

In talking about his books, *'Marketing Management'* (1967) and *'Marketing Decision-Making: a Model Building Approach'* (1970), Philip Kotler was asked:

> *'Were there any particular mentors in this?' He responded, 'I have always respected Ted Levitt at Harvard for his tremendous insights. And I learned a great deal from John Howard and Jagdish Sheth at Columbia who produced a very analytical view of consumer behaviour.'*

Sheth's views on industrial buying decisions

Organisational buying behaviour consists of:

1   the psychological aspect

2   the aspect relating to the conditions which precipitate joint decisions and

3   the aspect relating to the process of joint decision making with inevitable conflict among the decision-makers.

Many industrial buying decisions are made by people working in the purchasing, quality control and manufacturing departments. Their decisions are influenced by their expectations of suppliers and brands. These expectations, on the other hand, are influenced by the background of the individuals involved, the sources from which they get information, active search, perceptual distortion and satisfaction with past purchases.

Various studies reinforce the point that individual's perceptions and experiences vary and these perceptions and experiences influence decision making process.

> 'Not all industrial buying decisions are made jointly by the various individuals involved in the purchasing process.' **In some cases such decisions are delegated and it is important for the supplier to find out where and to whom the decisions are delegated.** 'There are six primary factors which determine whether a specific buying decision will be joint or autonomous. Of the six factors three relate to product-specific factors and the other three relate to company-specific factors.'

Sheth then goes on to explore the ways joint decisions are made and the conflict involved in making industrial buying decisions.

> 'Finally, it is important to realize that not all industrial decisions are the outcome of a systematic decision-making process. There are some industrial buying decisions which are based strictly on the set of situational factors for which theorizing or model-building will not be relevant or useful. What is needed in these cases is a check-list of empirical observations of the ad hoc events which vitiate the neat relationship between the theory or the model and a specific buying decision.'

Theories to explain the consumer behaviour process began in the mid-1960s. Jagdish Sheth together with John Howard was the first among leading theorists. Since 1960s there have been numerous researches on the marketing implications of the process. Also since Sheth's attempt to provide a comprehensive model of organisational buying behaviour, the emphasis has shifted to much more detailed analysis of how actual buying decisions are made and the precise nature of the factors affecting such decision-making.

Jagdish Sheth has been involved in making various contributions in the field of marketing for more than four decades now. He has contributed significantly in the field of telecom marketing and developing breakthrough relationships.

The following extracts come from: Jagdish Sheth and Andrew Sobel (2000). *'Clients For Life: How Great Professionals Develop Breakthrough Relationships'*. **Simon & Schuster.**

This book is aimed at professionals who want to develop long-term client relationships. The book develops what the authors call the 'developmental journey – from expert for hire to trusted adviser':

- Clients today are very discriminating and highly sophisticated and educated individuals.

- Some professionals are treated like vendors.

- Most professionals would like to be extraordinary consultants and provide value to their clients.

- The professionals are categorised into:

  1 service professions like lawyers, accountants, management consultants,

  2 sales executives – business consultants and

  3 staff and functional managers.

- Clients want their advisers to be good listeners, empathetic, have conviction, have good bedside manners, and people who can see the big picture.

- They highlight these three barriers to developing breakthrough relationships:

  1 Specialisation.

  2 Expertise is becoming automated and reduced to a commodity.

  3 Many professionals are held back by stereotypes about what clients want them to be and how they should behave.

- To create value for clients they present the following formula: **Insight x Collaborative Relationships = Client value**.

- The attributes that represent insight are: selfless independence, empathy, conviction, integrity, ability to think and reason, ability to synthesise, and judgement. These attributes contribute significantly to the professional's effectiveness.

'These are the qualities that foster the development and the insights and relationships that lead to consistent value creation for clients, and they are the characteristics that great advisers themselves have intuitively developed. If you want, in short, to become an extraordinary professional who commands unwavering client loyalty, you need especially to develop and strengthen these attributes.'

The content of this book and the subject matter reflects the agility of mind of Professor Sheth. He and his co-author have focused on clients as opposed to customers. They write:

'The distinction between a client and a customer is more than semantic. Customers, for example, buy a product or service with well-defined characteristics that match their needs, with little or no negotiation and discussion between buyer and seller; the professional's relationship with a client, in contrast, has a consultative aspect to it – there is a give-and-take to clarify needs, identify problems, and recommend solutions. While there doesn't have to be a personal relationship between a customer and the seller of the product or service, with a client there is typically a close, personal relationship with a high degree of trust. Finally a professional offers a client an authoritative body of knowledge and expertise...'

This book is very valuable in addressing the needs of clients – yet another dimension of present day marketing.

In his recent interview with Management First, he was asked about the impact of globalisation on marketing practice. His response included the point that globalisation was creating diverse communities and he said:

> 'There is no need to go out and test anything. There is sufficient cultural diversity in the USA to do a market test there. This development changes the whole nature of the way we do business.'

He also makes the point on segmentation in a diversified global market.

> 'take teenagers: all over the world they are the same so, if you sell MTV or if you sell rock 'n' roll music there are no difference between a Chinese teenager and a French, Indian or American teenager. You can, therefore, organise targeting by either local or global markets...'

> 'The other way to do it would take the opposite approach, ignoring consumer profiles because of the expense of targeting micro-segments. The solution here might be to adopt the approach of public policymakers, standardising the market and shaping market expectations.'

At the feet of Jagdish Sheth:
Lessons learnt:

- Understand the buying behaviour of your customers/ consumers.

- Collective buying behaviour is the result of many factors.

- Expectations and experience play key roles in buying behaviour.

- Do not consider collective buying behaviour to be the result of a systematic decision-making process.

- Professionals should discriminate between customers and clients.

- Provide value to your clients.

- Be good listeners.

- Empathise with your clients.

- Do not be blinkered by your specialism.

- Clients have personal and consultative relationships with professionals.

NINE
Thomas T. Nagle

Nagle on pricing

Thomas T. Nagle is a professor in the School of Management, Boston University and a President of the Strategic Pricing Group, Boston.

He made his mark from his publications on the subject of pricing.

His publications include:

Nagle Thomas T. (1987) '*The Strategy and Tactics of Pricing: A Guide to Profitable Decision Making*', Prentice Hall.

Nagle Thomas T and Holden Reed K. '*The Strategy and tactics of Pricing*', Prentice Hall.

Pricing is one of the four Ps of marketing. It did not gain much importance for marketers till 1970s when it came to be realised that pricing is not just about cost but it also incorporates perceived value by customers and competitive positioning.

The following extracts come from: Thomas T. Nagle: '*The Strategy and Tactics of Pricing: A Guide to Profitable Decision making*'. (1987). Prentice Hall.

'Marketing is a discipline of four coequal elements:

1   *the product,*

2   *its promotion*

3   *its distribution and*

4   *its pricing.*

The role which pricing plays in marketing strategy differs essentially from the roles of the other elements – product, promotion, and distribution – which are a firm's attempt to create value in the marketplace. Pricing is the firm's attempt to capture some of the value in the profits it earns. If effective product development, promotion, and distribution sow the seeds of business success, effective pricing is the harvest. While effective pricing can never compensate for poor execution of the first three elements, ineffective pricing can surely prevent those efforts from resulting in financial success. Regrettably, that is a common occurrence.'

Many companies fail to price effectively because they do not adopt marketing perspective in their pricing strategy. It is important to understand how customers make their buying decisions in order to formulate effective pricing.

Pricing strategy should involve external perspective as opposed to internal perspective, i.e. looking at its own internal needs.

Nagle examines two methods of cost-based pricing – mark up pricing and target-return pricing – and shows how such an internal focus deviates from meeting market needs.

Effective pricing should consider:

- Consumer behaviour

- Co-ordinating pricing with new product development.

- Understanding a product's pricing environment. Understand likely action of competitors.

- Understanding costs and the issues involved in relation to organisation's costs. What costs are incremental, or forward-looking or avoidable?

- Understanding price sensitivity. The factors affecting price sensitivity are:

  1 They are consumer or purchaser's value, For those who have studied Economics this is the question of utility and marginal utility of consumers;

  2 availability and attributes of substitutes;

  3 difficulties in comparing substitutes;

  4 total expenditure;

  5 the end-benefit;

  6 the shared cost;

  7 the sunk investment effect – many purchasers are used in conjunction with assets bought previously.

  8 The price-quality effect and

  9 the inventory effect.

Competition changes the nature of pricing. There are four types of prices which are identified in the context of competition. These are cooperative pricing, adaptive pricing, opportunistic pricing and predatory pricing.

> 'The challenge facing a pricing strategist is to analyse the reasons for its competitors' pricing in order to better anticipate how they will price in the future.'

To respond to a specific environment, three types of pricing are considered, these are *skim pricing, penetration pricing* and *neutral pricing*.

The rest of the book focuses on pricing over the product life cycle, segmented pricing, pricing in the marketing mix, establishing foundations for more profitable pricing, psychological aspects of pricing and pricing with uncertainty.

Nagle's book is a must-read book for those who want to understand the nature of pricing and its importance in marketing mix.

Kotler in his book 'Principles of Marketing' quotes Nagle on pricing:

'Pricing requires more than technical expertise. It requires creative judgement and an awareness of buyers' motivation... The key to effective pricing is the same one that open doors... in other marketing functions: a creative awareness of who buyers are, why they buy, and how they make their buying decisions. The recognition that buyers differ in these dimensions is as important for effective pricing as it is for effective promotion, distribution, or product development.'[31]

He also reinforces Nagle's point that good pricing begins with analysing consumer needs and price perceptions. Price must be considered along with the other marketing-mix variables before the marketing programme is set.

In his article 'Pricing as Creative Marketing', Nagle writes:

'The actual task of pricing falls, however, distinctly and rightly in the domain of marketing because pricing requires more than mere technical expertise. It requires creative judgement and a keen awareness of buyers' motivations. Consequently, the specific strategies of successful pricing are as varied as the imaginations of creative individuals. But what they all have in common is recognition of differences among buyers....'

At the feet of Thomas Nagle: Lessons learnt

- Pricing is one of the key elements in the marketing mix.

- Pricing incorporates perceived value by customers.

- Adopt marketing perspective to pricing.

- Competition changes the nature of pricing.

- Pricing should fall in marketing domain.

TEN
Gurus and strategic analytical tools

In marketing, various analytical tools are used to facilitate decision-making. Some of the tools have been made popular by 'gurus' and some by 'organisations'. This chapter will deal with some of the tools which all students of marketing have to be conversant with.

Caution: Please note that none of the tools are 'perfect' in that they do not provide a panacea for diagnosis and decision. All the tools require judgement and experience in their application.

Ansoff's Matrix

Dr. Igor Ansoff, known as the father of strategic management, died on July 14, 2002. He was a 'heavy weight' guru of strategy and is known for coining the term 'strategic management'. His first book, *'Corporate Strategy'* was published in 1965.

His other books include *'Business Strategy'* (1969), *'Strategic Management'* (1984). *'The Firm: Meeting the Legacy Challenge'* (1986). *'The New Corporate Strategy'* (1989) and more than 150 published articles.

He has had a profound influence in the field of strategic management and thinking. In relation to marketing he is famous for his matrix, a well-known marketing tool, which was first published in Harvard Business Review in 1957.

The matrix offers strategic choices facing managers in order to achieve their objectives. The matrix involves two dimensions, namely product and market. There are four permutations. These are:

1   Existing product/existing market.

2   New product/existing market.

3   Existing product/new market.

4   New product/new market.

In each of these situations there are strategic choices presented on which to take action.

Existing product/existing market: In this situation a company has an option of either doing nothing, which means continuing its existing strategy or to choose to consolidate its current market position by focusing attention and initiating marketing activities in the area where it has competitive advantage or to choose to penetrate the market (market penetration). Revenues could be increased by promoting the product or the brand. In static or declining markets, a firm will face intense competition to gain market share. Market penetration would normally involve expenditure in support of price discounts, distribution incentives etc.

New product/existing market

In this situation, the company has to invest in introducing new products to its existing market. The focus is to build on the existing knowledge to explore new opportunities identified by the company. Over time all products pass through a product life cycle. As existing products mature, new developments are often introduced to extend the product life cycle. An example of such a strategy would be Unilever's introduction of the three-in-one dishwasher tablets which replaced the need for separate salt, detergent and rinse agents.

Existing product/new market

Here the company has to market its existing product in a new market. This is the strategy of market development. The strategy also involves promoting new uses for an existing product and market segments.

Market development can be achieved through identifying potential user groups in the current market areas or seeking additional distribution channels in the present geographical locations.

Generally speaking, market development strategy is less risky than product development because the company can rely on the current activity level of the existing product in the market whilst it pursues new market opportunities. McDonalds, for example, a US fast food chain has adopted a market development strategy through franchising in many parts of the world.

New product/new market

In this situation the company has to pursue diversification strategy. Diversification can either be horizontal, vertical or conglomerate.

Horizontal diversification refers to the development of activities which are complementary to the company's existing activities. Nestle's takeover of Rowntree Mackintosh is an example of horizontal diversification.

Vertical diversification refers to the development of activities which involve the stages in the company's value chain. Downward integration, for example, would involve the company's activity related to the preceding stage of its production process whereas upward integration would involve its succeeding stage in the production process.

Conglomerate diversification happens when a company seeks new businesses that have no relationship to its current technology, products or markets.

Ansoff's matrix enables businesses to look at their products and markets and to think of appropriate strategies for their business.

Porter's Generic Competitive Strategies

Michael Porter, strategy guru, presented his generic strategies for businesses to consider relating to winning and sustaining competitive advantage. These strategies are **cost leadership** (the firm sets out to become the low cost producer in its sector), **differentiation** (where a firm seeks to be unique in its sector) and **focus** (focusing on specific segments). This is explained in some detail in chapter four.

Boston Consulting Group – Product Portfolio Matrix

This matrix has been devised by a consulting firm rather than an individual guru. This matrix is used in product portfolio planning, and many marketing gurus and writers including Philip Kotler refer to it in their writings.

The focus of the matrix is on market growth and relative market share.

Each strategic business unit has to determine its annual growth rate in the market. This rate could be either 'high' (say 10 per cent) or 'low' (say 2 per cent).

Each business unit has to determine its relative market share. This could be 'high' market share or 'low' market share.

The strategic business units are then positioned in the matrix according to the information provided. These strategic business units are then classified as 'cash cows' or 'dogs' or 'problem children' or 'stars'.

Low growth/high share

The strategic business unit under this category would be a 'cash cow'. Such products generate more revenue than they use and surplus revenue can be used to finance other products or other strategic business units.

Low growth/low share

The strategic business unit under this category is classified as a 'dog'. These are products with a low share of a low growth market. The products or strategic business units tend to be loss-makers.

High growth/low share

The strategic business unit under this classification is referred as a 'problem child' because they consume lots of resources but generate low return. They are products with possible long term potential.

High growth/high share

The strategic business unit under this position is classified as a 'star' because they generate good income in the face of competition and they need to be maintained as they have potential of becoming future cash cows.

This matrix is over-simplified and does not consider other factors impacting on strategic business units and products. There is also a debate as to what constitutes high or low market growth rate or relative market share.

Katherine Harrigan, a professor at Harvard Business School and a strategy guru, believes that 'dogs' can hold value in the market place. In her book 'Managing Maturing Business' (1988), she presents 'end-game strategies' in this situation. The two dimensions used for her matrix are industry structure and competitive strength.

LEADERSHIP

When there are competitive strengths in attractive niches and a favourable industry structure and market conditions, then investment should be undertaken to acquire a leadership position in the market place.

NICHE

Where the business has a relative competitive strength in attractive niches and there is a favourable industry structure and demand conditions, then the business should pull out of the broad market and focus on niches.

QUICK SALE

Where there are no competitive strengths in attractive niches and there is an unfavourable industry structure and demand conditions, the business should seek a quick sale to capitalise on existing value.

HARVEST

Harvesting assumes that value can be returned to a business by continuing to run it to extract as much cash as possible.

In declining industries, according to Harrigan, the companies can either fight by choosing to assume leadership or niche position or flee by adopting a quick sale or harvesting strategies.

General Electric Strategic Planning Matrix

Because there are multiple factors affecting businesses, General Electric working with McKinsey & Co. has developed a multi factor approach to business portfolio analysis.

Each business is rated in terms of two major dimensions. They are market attractiveness and business strength. The factors underlying market attractiveness are overall market size, annual market growth-rate, historical profit margin, and competitive intensity, technological requirements, vulnerability to inflation, energy requirements, environmental impact and sociological, technological, economic and political factors. The factors underlying business strength are market share, share growth, product quality, brand reputation, distribution network, promotional effectiveness, productive capacity, productive efficiency, unit costs, material supplies, R & D performance and managerial personnel.

The matrix is divided into nine cells (see over) representing the following positions:

- Business strength (**BS**): Strong, medium and weak.

- Market attractiveness (**MA**): High, medium and low.

The nine cells of the General Electric Strategic Planning Matrix

1	**BS strong, MA high:**	Invest to grow.
2	**BS medium, MA high:**	Invest to build and reinforce vulnerable areas.
3	**BS weak, MA high:**	Build selectively. Capitalise on strengths and minimise any weaknesses.
4	**BS strong, MA medium:**	Invest in attractive segments.
5	**BS medium, MA medium:**	Focus on segments where profit is good.
6	**BS weak, MA medium:**	Limited expansion or harvest.
7	**BS strong, MA low:**	Manage for current earnings.
8	**BS medium, MA low:**	Protect positions in most profitable segments.
9	**BS weak, MA low:**	Divest.

The above is adapted from Kotler 'Marketing Management' book.

The GE matrix, because it deals with multi factors offers significant improvement over the Boston Consulting Group matrix. The problem in practice is to assign appropriate weighting to each factor affecting business strength and market attractiveness.

Shell Directional Policy Matrix

Shell developed an approach similar to GE Matrix. Their matrix has two dimensions, namely the company's competitive capabilities (**CC**) and prospects for sector profitability (**PSP**).

There are various factors affecting these two dimensions. There are also nine positions in this matrix. They are:

1	**PSP unattractive, CC strong:**	Cash generation opportunity.
2	**PSP average, CC strong:**	Growth and leadership opportunity.
3	**PSP attractive, CC strong:**	Leadership opportunity.
4	**PSP unattractive, CC average:**	Phased withdrawal.
5	**PSP average, CC average:**	Growth opportunity.
6	**PSP attractive, CC average:**	Try harder.
7	**PSP Unattractive, CC weak:**	Disinvest.
8	**PSP average, CC weak:**	Phased withdrawal.
9	**PSP attractive, CC weak:**	Double or quit.

To quote Kotler:[32]

'The models have helped managers to think more futuristically and strategically, to understand the economics of their businesses better, to improve the quality of their plans, to improve communication between business and corporate management, to pinpoint information gaps and important issues, and to eliminate weaker businesses and strengthen their investment in more promising businesses.

On the other hand, portfolio models must be used cautiously. They may lead the company to place too much emphasis on the market-share growth and entry into high-growth businesses, to the neglect of managing the current businesses well. The results are sensitive to the ratings and weights and can be manipulated to produce a desired location in the matrix...'

SWOT (Strengths, Weaknesses, Opportunities and Threats) analysis

This approach, which has been explained by Ansoff and Kotler, involves analysing the strengths, weaknesses, opportunities and threats facing businesses.

In order to succeed, businesses need to understand what their strengths are and where they are vulnerable. They need this assessment of their internal resources and capabilities in order to take advantage of opportunities in the market place and to face the challenges from competitors and the outside environment. Businesses have to aim to achieve 'strategic fit'.

Strengths

Looking inside your organisation considers what strengths you have in relation to your resources and capabilities, structure, culture, leadership, products, systems, values and processes.

Weaknesses

What weaknesses do you have in relation to the above factors? Consider what is done badly and what could be avoided. What are the key bottlenecks etc?

Opportunities

In scanning the external environment (see next section), and having undertaken industry analysis (Porter's Five Forces Framework), what opportunities do you see available to your business? What trends and changes are there in the environment?

Threats

In looking outside your business:

- What challenges do you face and how you are going to face them?

- Is changing technology threatening your business?

- Note that strengths and weaknesses relate generally to factors inside your organisation whereas opportunities and threats relate to factors outside your organisation.

According to Grant,[33] the SWOT framework is handicapped by difficulties in distinguishing strengths from weaknesses and opportunities from threats....

The lesson here is that an arbitrary classification of external factors into opportunities and threats, and internal factors into strengths and weaknesses, is less important than a careful identification of these external and internal factors followed by an appraisal of their implications.

Scanning the external environment: (STEP) factors

Scanning the external environment has always been an important issue in strategy. Ansoff and Kotler and other strategy and marketing gurus have underlined the need for scanning the wider environment. Ansoff, for example, advocated identifying strong signals (an example would be sudden recession) and weak signals (for example, ageing population) in strategic planning.

Scanning the marketing environment enables businesses to identify opportunities and threats in the market place. Businesses operate and make decisions within the context of the macroeconomic environment.

According to Philip Kotler there are four levels of environment which provide a context to all businesses. They are:

The task environment. This consists of key players such as suppliers, distributors and customers who have a direct impact on businesses.

The competitive environment. This consists of key competitors.

The public environment. This consists of institutions which regulate the activities of the organisation.

The macro-environment which consists of sociological, technological, economic and political factors (STEP factors).

The **STEP analysis** (sometimes known as PEST analysis) enables organisations to assess the changes that impact the business:

Sociological factors (S)

Sociological factors relate to changes taking place in a society. These changes apply to social attitudes, social values, and changes in the educational system, life styles, structure of household, ageing population etc. In some societies, for example, it took a long time to convince people to use condoms to exercise family planning.

Demographic changes such as birth rates, population size, age structure and population mobility affect human resources and marketing strategies of companies.

Technological factors (T)

New technologies and skills are becoming increasingly diffused world-wide and more and more businesses are becoming high-tech. For example, South Korean companies were renowned once for producing cheap and shoddy goods such as shoes and textiles. Now they are known for producing high-tech high-quality goods. The push was led by leading producers like Samsung and Hyundai.

Technological developments are taking place at a breathtaking place specifically in the telecommunications and entertainment industries. Advances in technologies will intensify competition. The convergence of computing, communication and information will lead to a global information superhighway which will expand markets, develop new businesses and increase competition.

The emergence of the internet has also transformed the business landscape. It has been said that no technology in history has spread faster than the internet. Its biggest impact is speed. It delivers speed of deliberations, transactions and information. It creates a market where buyers and sellers come together. Cisco, it is reported, sold $5 billion in goods over the internet in 1998.

Economic factors (E)

Economic factors such as wealth distribution, purchasing power, economic growth, consumer spending, inflation, unemployment, interest rates etc. are all key determinants of demand.

One of the most sensitive issues for many businesses today is the level of interest rates. At present in the United Kingdom the interest-rate is the lowest it has been for over four decades.

Another key economic factor impacting on competition is exchange rates. Fluctuations in exchange rates affect exports and imports. Arguments and discussions are still going on in relation to the fixing of exchange rates within the European Union and the UK joining single currency 'club'.

The past two decades have also seen a revolution as domestic financial markets have been opened up to create a massive global capital market. This change has contributed to the explosive growth of the financial markets. A 'free' capital market ensures that savings are directed to the most productive investments without regard for national boundaries.

Political factors (P)

Politically the climate is changing from conflict to co-operation. Geographic boundaries are ceasing to be barriers to trade and competition. Privatisation and de-regulation have been the main drivers in opening up the global market.

Since the fall of the Berlin Wall and the abandonment of communism in many countries there have been steady streams of acquisitions, alliances, strategic partnerships and supplier networks.

Enlargement of the European Union also has taken on board countries that formerly created barriers to trade for dogmatic reasons.

Since the event of September 11 and the declaration of war on terrorism, countries are now forming 'alliances' to combat terrorism.

STEP factors influence significantly the way we do business today. The STEP factors are inter-related. Fahey and Narayanan (1986)[34] stress that the environment can only be understood as a system in which each factor is related to and affects every other factor.

STEP factors and your business

Under each category – sociological, technological, economic and political – identify factors appropriate to your business. Identify key variables and assess their probability of change and the consequent impact of that change on your business in terms of your revenue, profitability, market and competition. Priority in terms of taking action should be focused on high probability of change with high impact on your business. Consider various scenarios for your business in formulating marketing strategy.

Scenario planning

Scenario Planning helps organisations manage uncertainty and make better decisions. It was originally developed within Royal Dutch Shell which made the practice famous by using it to anticipate the Arab oil embargo and also anticipate and prepare for the dramatic drop in oil prices during the 1980s. It deals with the creation of multiple alternative futures, representing situations that could reasonably occur.

According to Peter Schwartz[35], a scenario planning guru, 'Using scenarios is rehearsing the future. You run through the simulated events as if you were already living them. You train yourself to recognise which drama is unfolding. That helps you avoid unpleasant surprises, and know how to act.'

Scenario planning is like reading the weather: it may rain or snow; there will be some sun and some light showers. Scenario planning requires us to assume a 'what if' mindset, pliable enough to come up with flexible strategies to accommodate multiple futures.

Dos and Don'ts in Scenario Planning

DO

- Scan the external environment.

- Analyse the external factors that impact on the nature of your business.

- Construct various scenarios using external factors as your context.

- Create multiple futures facing your business.

- Question your mental models.

- Plan for and anticipate surprises.

- Adopt a multi-disciplinary approach.

- Assume 'what if' mindset.

- Involve all staff.

- Formulate strategies associated with each scenario.

- Work out the action plan associated with each scenario.

DON'T

- Embark on the exercise of scenario building without conviction or commitment.

- Consider scenario building as a window-dressing exercise.

- Get stuck into one best strategy.

- Work on existing assumptions.

- Prepare a plan without specifying who should what and when.

- Conduct a scenario-building exercise as a one-off event.

Benchmarking

According to Philip Kotler[36]:

> *'Companies normally learn about their competitors' strengths and weaknesses through secondary data, personal experience, and hearsay. They can augment their knowledge by conducting primary marketing research with customers, suppliers and dealers. A growing number of companies are turning to benchmarking as the best guide to improving their competitive standing.'*

What is benchmarking?

Benchmarking is a method of improving business performance by learning from other organisations how to do things better in order to be the 'best in the class'. The aim of a benchmarking is to improve upon the best practices of other organisations.

Benchmarking originated in the USA in the late 1970s. Now 95 per cent of US companies say they are practising it. As far as Europe is concerned benchmarking seems to be well established. Coopers & Lybrand undertook a survey in 1994 covering The Times 1000 companies or their equivalent across five European countries: the United Kingdom, the Netherlands, Switzerland, Spain and France. The survey defined benchmarking as 'the process of comparing business practices and performance levels between companies (or divisions within companies) in order to gain new insights and to identify opportunities for making improvements.

The survey showed that over two-thirds of companies in the United Kingdom, the Netherlands and Switzerland, over half of French companies and a third of Spanish companies are using benchmarking techniques. Benchmarking is used across all of the principal business functions.

There are various types of benchmarking. These include competitive benchmarking (benchmarking against your competitors), strategic benchmarking, process benchmarking, product benchmarking, customer service benchmarking and internal benchmarking.

How to benchmark

- Identify the subject to benchmark.
- Identify the best practice.
- Collect data.
- Analyse and determine current gaps.
- Project future performance.
- Communicate results.
- Establish goals.
- Develop an action plan.
- Implement plan.
- Monitor results and recalibrate the benchmark.

Advantages of benchmarking

- Provides direction and impetus for improvement.
- Promotes competitive awareness.
- Becomes the stepping stone to breakthrough thinking.
- Identifies the best practice.
- Links operational tactics to corporate vision and strategy.
- Challenges the 'status quo'. Allows realistic stretch goals.

ELEVEN
Further information

Suggested reading

Always acquire the latest editions.

- Baker, Michael. *'Marketing: An Introductory Text'* (1971). Macmillan.

- Day, George. *'Strategic Market Planning: The Pursuit of Competitive Advantage'*. (1984) West Publishing

- Davidson, Hugh, and J. *'Offensive Marketing: How to make your competitors followers'*. (1987). Gower.

- Drucker: *'The Practice of Management'* (1955). Heinemann.

- Drucker: *'The Effective Executive'* (1967). Heinemann.

- Enis, Ben M. and Cox, Keith K. *'Marketing Classics: A selection of Influential Articles'*. (1988). Allyn and bacon Inc.

- Evans, Joel R. and Berman, Barry. *'Marketing'* (1982) Collier Macmillan.

- Grundy, Tony. *'Gurus on Strategy'*. (2003). Thorogood.

- Keegan, Warren. *'Global Marketing Management'*. (1974). Prentice Hall.

- Keegan, Warren. *'Multinational marketing Management'*. (1974). Prentice Hall.

- Kermally, Sultan. *'Total Management Thinking: Ideas that are Transforming Management'*. (1996). Butterworth-Heinemann.

- Kotler, Philip: *'Principles of Marketing'* (1994). Prentice Hall.

- Kotler, Philip. *'Marketing management: Analysis, Planning, Implementation, and Control'*. (1994). Prentice Hall.

- Kotler, Philip. *'Marketing For Non-profit Organizations'*. (1982) Prentice Hall.

- Kotler, Philip and Paul, Bloom: *'Marketing Professional service'* (1984). Prentice Hall.

- Kotler, Philip and Cox, Keith K. *'Marketing Management and Strategy – A Reader'*. (1988). Prentice Hall.

- Levitt, Theodore. *'The Marketing Imagination'* (1983). The Free Press.

- McDonald, Malcolm(Ed). *'Marketing strategies: New Approaches, New Techniques.'* (1995). Pergamon.

- McDonald, Malcolm and Payne, Adian. *'Marketing Planning for Services'*. (1996). Butterworth Heinemann.

- Micklethwait, John and Wooldridge, Adrian. *'The Witch Doctors – What the management Gurus are saying, Why it matters and How to make sense of it.'* (1996). Heinemann.

- Nagle, Thomas. *'The Strategy and tactics of Pricing'*. (1987) Prentice Hall.

- Peters and Waterman Jr. *'In Search of Excellence: Lessons from America's Best-Run Companies.'* (1982). Harper and Row.

- Peters, Tom: *'Liberation management: Necessary Disorganisation For the Nanosecond Nineties.'* (1992) Macmillan.

- Peters, Tom: *'The Pursuit of Wow!'*(1992). Vintage Books.

- Peters, Tom. *'Thriving on Chaos'* (1987). Alfred A. Knopf.

- Porter, Michael. *'Competitive Strategy: Techniques for Analyzing Industries and Competitors'*. (1980) the Free Press.

- Porter, Michael: *'Competitive Advantage: Creating and Sustaining Superior Performance'*. (1985). the Free Press.

- Sheth, Jagdish and Sobel, Andrew. *'Clients for Life'*. (2000). Simon & Schuster.

- Treacy, Michael and Wiersema. *'Discipline of Market Leaders'*. (1995).

- Addison-Wesley. *'Best Practice Marketing'* (1994). The Economist Intelligence Unit.

- Wilmshurst, John. *'The Fundamentals of Marketing'*. (1978) Heinemann.

- Zikmund and D Amico. *'Marketing'*. (1984). John Wiley.

Useful websites

- http://www.business2.org.uk

- http://www.harvardbusinessonline.hbsp.harvard.edu

- http://www.marketingpower.com

- http://www.marketing.org

- http://www.cim.co.uk

- http://www.brint.com

- http://www.fitforthefuture.com

- http://www.dti.gov.uk

- http://www.businessexcellence.co.uk

- http://www.best-in-class.com

References

1   Murphy, P. E. and Enis, B. M. (1986) *Classifying products strategically*. Journal of marketing, July.

2   Jagdish N. Sheth (Guru Interview). Management First. 7th February, 2003.

3   Kotler, P. (1972) *A generic concept of marketing*. Journal of Marketing, April.

4   Kotler, Philip and Armstrong Gary (sixth edition) *Principles of Marketing*. Prentice Hall, p11.

5   Theodore Levitt (1986) *The Marketing Imagination*, p153. The Free Press.

6   Ward et al (1999). *What high-tech managers need know about brands.* Harvard Business Review, July-Aug, pp85. © The President and Fellows of the Harvard College: all rights reserved.

7   Joel R. Evans/Barry Berman (1985). *Marketing* second edition, p311.

8   Peters and Waterman (1982) *In Search of Excellence*. Harper and Row.

9   Macdonald, Malcolm, H. B. (1984). *Marketing Plans: How to prepare them, how to use them*. Heinemann, p11-12.

10 Levitt (1986). *The Marketing Imagination*. The Free Press, p24.

11 Keegan (1974) *Global Marketing Management* Sixth Edition. Prentice Hall, p7 and 23.

12 Micklethwait, John and Wooldridge, Adrian. *Witch Doctors. what the management gurus are saying, why it matters and how to make sense of it* (1996). Heinemann, p71.

13 Theodore Levitt: *The Marketing Imagination* (1986). The Free Press, p153.

14 Drucker, Peter, *'Innovation and Entrepreneurship'*. (1985). Heinemann.

15 David Schmittlein, *'Customer as strategic assets'*. Mastering Management Part 8. Financial Times.

16 Theodore Levitt. *'Marketing Imagination'* (1983), p143.

17 Ibid, p148.

18 Ibid, p152.

19 Ibid, p162.

20 Harvard Business Review vol. 54 (January-February, 1976), p102-112

21 *'Marketing Success through Differentiation – of Anything'*. © 1976, by the President and Fellows of Harvard College: all rights reserved.

22 Theodore Levitt: *'Marketing Success through Differentiation – of Anything'*. January-February, 1980. © 1980 by the President and Fellows of Harvard College: all rights reserved, p83-91.

23 See reference 12, p163.

24 Source: Grant, Robert M. (1991). *'Contemporary Strategy Analysis'*. Blackwell, p235.

25 Grant, p220

26 Keegan, Warren. *'Global Marketing Management'* (1999). Prentice Hall, p319.

27 Kotler Philip, Bloom Paul N. *'Marketing Professional services'*. (1984) Prentice Hall, p2.

28 See reference 12, p91.

29 See reference 12, p94.

30 Regis McKenna (1986).'*The Regis Touch*'. Addison Wesley-Publishing.

31 Thomas T. Nagle: '*Pricing as Creative Marketing*'. Business Horizons, July-August 1983, p19.

32 Kotler P. '*Marketing Management*' (eight editions) p75-76.

33 Grant, Robert M. '*Contemporary Strategy Analysis*' (Third Edition), p 12-13.

34 Fahey, L. and Narayanan V. K. (1986) '*Macro-environmental Analysis for Strategic Management*', p24-34.

35 The Economist Conferences Scenario Planning Seminar. 19 February, 1993.

36 Kotler (Eight Editions). '*Marketing Management: Analysis, Planning, Implementation, and Control.*' Prentice Hall, p233.

Thorogood publishing

Thorogood publishes a wide range of books, reports, special briefings and psychometric tests. Listed below is a selection of key titles.

Desktop Guides

The marketing strategy desktop guide   *Norton Paley* • £16.99

The sales manager's desktop guide
                              Mike Gale and Julian Clay • £16.99

The company director's desktop guide   *David Martin* • £16.99

The credit controller's desktop guide   *Roger Mason* • £16.99

The company secretary's desktop guide   *Roger Mason* • £16.99

The finance and accountancy desktop guide   *Ralph Tiffin* • £16.99

The commercial engineer's desktop guide   *Tim Boyce* • £16.99

The training manager's desktop guide   *Eddie Davies* • £16.99

The PR practitioner's desktop guide   *Caroline Black* • £16.99

Win new business – the desktop guide   *Susan Croft* • £16.99

Masters in Management

Mastering business planning and strategy   *Paul Elkin* • £14.99

Mastering financial management   *Stephen Brookson* • £14.99

Mastering leadership   *Michael Williams* • £14.99

Mastering negotiations   *Eric Evans* • £14.99

Mastering people management   *Mark Thomas* • £14.99

Mastering personal and interpersonal skills   *Peter Haddon* •£14.99

Mastering project management   *Cathy Lake* • £14.99

Business Action Pocketbooks

Edited by David Irwin

Building your business pocketbook   £6.99

Developing yourself and your staff pocketbook   £6.99

Finance and profitability pocketbook   £6.99

Managing and employing people pocketbook   £6.99

Sales and marketing pocketbook   £6.99

Managing projects and operations pocketbook   £6.99

Effective business communications pocketbook   £6.99

PR techniques that work   *Edited by Jim Dunn* • £6.99

Adair on leadership   *Edited by Neil Thomas* • £6.99

Other titles

The John Adair handbook of management and leadership
Edited by Neil Thomas • £24.99

The inside track to successful management
Dr Gerald Kushel • £12.99

The pension trustee's handbook (3rd edition)
Robin Ellison • £25

Boost your company's profits *Barrie Pearson* • £12.99

Negotiate to succeed *Julie Lewthwaite* • £12.99

The management tool kit *Sultan Kermally* • £10.99

Working smarter *Graham Roberts-Phelps* • £14.99

Test your management skills *Michael Williams* • £15.99

The art of headless chicken management
Elly Brewer and Mark Edwards • £6.99

EMU challenge and change – the implications for business
John Atkin • £11.99

Everything you need for an NVQ in management
Julie Lewthwaite • £22.99

Customer relationship management
Graham Roberts-Phelps • £14.99

Time management and personal development
John Adair and Melanie Allen • £10.99

Sales management and organisation *Peter Green* • £9.99

Telephone tactics *Graham Roberts-Phelps* • £10.99

Companies don't succeed people do!
Graham Roberts-Phelps • £12.99

Inspiring leadership	*John Adair* • £15.99
The book of ME	*Barrie Pearson and Neil Thomas* • £14.99
The complete guide to debt recovery	*Roger Mason* • £12.99
Janner's complete speechmaker	*Greville Janner* • £10.99
Gurus on business strategy	*Tony Grundy* • £14.99
Dynamic practice development	*Kim Tasso* • £29.99

Thorogood also has an extensive range of reports and special briefings which are written specifically for professionals wanting expert information.

For a full listing of all Thorogood publications, or to order any title, please call Thorogood Customer Services on 020 7749 4748 or fax on 020 7729 6110. Alternatively view our website at www.thorogood.ws.